Thank you to my many colleagues and to my family,
with whom I get to experiment and learn.
—Mike Rother

I'm privileged to work with a number of companies who are
kindly willing to experiment and learn together.
And I am particularly grateful to my family, where our three
children coach my wife, Mariecke, and me every day.
—Gerd Aulinger

Our special thanks to Mark Rosenthal
and Professor Jeffrey Liker.

TOYOTA KATA CULTURE

MIKE ROTHER
AND
GERD AULINGER

ILLUSTRATIONS BY LIBBY WAGNER

Mc
Graw
Hill
Education

NEW YORK   CHICAGO   SAN FRANCISCO   ATHENS
LONDON   MADRID   MEXICO CITY   MILAN
NEW DELHI   SINGAPORE   SYDNEY   TORONTO

1 2 3 4 5 6 7 8 9   LMN   22 21 20 19 18 17

ISBN 978-1-259-86044-7
MHID   1-259-86044-2

e-ISBN 978-1-259-86045-4
e-MHID   1-259-86045-0

Design by Mauna Eichner and Lee Fukui
Illustrations by Libby Wagner, MPS North America

Library of Congress Cataloging-in-Publication Data

Names: Rother, Mike, author. | Aulinger, Gerd, author.
Title: Toyota kata culture : building organizational capability and mindset
  through kata coaching / Mike Rother and Gerd Aulinger.
Description: New York : McGraw-Hill, 2017.
Identifiers: LCCN 2016054901 (print) | LCCN 2017006805 (ebook) | ISBN
  9781259860447 (alk. paper) | ISBN 1259860442 | ISBN 9781259860454 () |
  ISBN 1259860450
Subjects: LCSH: Total quality management. | Organizational behavior. |
  Corporate culture.
Classification: LCC HD62.15 .R6849 2017 (print) | LCC HD62.15 (ebook) | DDC
  658.4/013--dc23
LC record available at https://lccn.loc.gov/2016054901

McGraw-Hill Education books are available at special quantity discounts to use as premiums and sales promotions or for use in corporate training programs. To contact a representative, please visit the Contact Us pages at www.mhprofessional .com.

We never know exactly what steps
will lead to our goals, but we can practice
and learn *how to reach goals.*

FOREWORD

by Professor Jeffrey K. Liker

This is the first book I have read that provides a clear picture of what it takes to develop and mobilize creative capability across an organization, to achieve challenging goals.

Toyota has been using something called policy deployment annually since the 1960s to align improvement activities toward company-level challenges. It works, but all their internal charts about policy deployment include two little acronyms that Toyota believes are necessary to make it work—PS and OJD. "PS" refers to problem solving, which is the scientific approach for turning your level's objectives into a meaningful plan and then iteratively working toward improving processes to achieve these objectives. "OJD" refers to on-the-job development, which is the way your manager coaches you day by day to develop the skills for scientific PS.

Without these competencies, policy deployment outside Toyota became just cascaded objectives for everyone to make the numbers however they could. The easiest path between your current situation and making the numbers is a straight line. Find things you already know how to implement and do them. Managers have been doing this since the dawn of bureaucracy, and they do make the numbers, but with little innovation and little real improvement in how the work gets done. That's dangerous for any organization in the long run. Today we know that Toyota's secret to driving real improvement, real thoughtful improvement, is PS and OJD. But this still begs the question: How do we do PS and OJD?

In *Toyota Kata* (2009), Mike Rother gave us a critical piece of the puzzle we were missing. He introduced a clear and actionable approach to developing these competencies in real people, especially those who do not work for Toyota, so that the skills for continuous improvement become habitual. It turns out that there is a general approach for developing complex skills of any kind, which we have known about for centuries, and it applies equally well to developing the skills for improvement. If you want to know what that is, glance in at a piano lesson or watch a good coach teach their players. What has evolved over many years is a way of developing skilled musicians or athletes or artists or cooks or you name it, through deliberate practice.

Step one is to define what mastery means. In the case of Toyota-style Lean, Rother defined mastery as a scientific approach to improvement, which, by the way, the master teachers at Toyota have been saying about the Toyota Production System for over 70 years. Step two is to break down any complex skill into teachable pieces, which in the martial arts are called "Kata." Kata are small routines or drills that, when practiced repeatedly, with a coach to correct deviations, generate new abilities and mindset. Think of the basic three-step pattern of dancing a waltz. At the beginning you have to master this by counting 1-2-3 and moving your feet in the proper way consciously. A scientific approach to improvement also requires fundamental skills that only become natural through practice.

The practice routines of the Improvement Kata are designed to help you develop scientific thinking skills. There are practice routines for understanding the direction, grasping the current condition, establishing the next short-term target condition to innovate toward, and then for experimenting to achieve that target condition. There are even Kata for the coach to practice, to learn how to provide corrective feedback without shutting down the learner.

The first step in the Improvement Kata is understanding the direction. This starts at the top with strategy, which is usually more than just cutting costs by some percent. What do we need to become in the next X number of years to better serve customers and beat our competition? It could be a new breakthrough product, it could be the fastest lead time in the industry, or it could be providing a level of service that customers have not yet seen.

The strategy gets broken down into an overall challenge for the business. This, in turn, gets broken down at each level, to challenges appropriate for that level. The challenge for sales will be different from the challenge for product development, which will be different from the challenge for operations. This gets figured out through back and forth coach/learner dialogues, like the ones shown in this book.

Once the direction is clear the magic happens, and the magic is not simply sprinting to the finish line. It is thoughtfully designing and running rapid experiments to iteratively learn your way to a new level of performance in the direction of the challenge. Teach the ability to do this at all levels of the organization and your capacity for delivering value to customers multiplies.

The chain of coaching that's vividly illustrated in this book is what policy deployment should be, but rarely is. Without the Improvement Kata and Coaching Kata, few organizations have even a vision of what translating a deployed policy into real improvement looks like in practice. With the Kata, we have a means to go beyond a vision, to the skills required for actual practice.

If it seems I am excited about this it is because I am. I have been preaching for decades about how policy deployment is as much a people development approach as it is a way of getting the most critical results for the business. I have been preaching the importance of the process of translating business goals into meaningful objectives and measures at all levels and across the organization. And then experimenting to learn your way to these objectives. I can describe how Toyota does this, but that would not present a clear way to develop the competencies needed to make this real in your organization. And here it is! Read about it, think about it, get the picture. Then take your journey in a new direction based on strategic thinking and scientific execution. All it takes is the first practice step, and the next, and the next.

Ann Arbor, Michigan, USA
January 2017

CONTENTS

FROM KATA TO CULTURE

Toyota Kata Culture shows you how to scale up individual practice of the Improvement Kata and Coaching Kata across an entire organization, to create *team* scientific thinking capabilities that can be applied to any challenging objective.

Scientific thinking is perhaps the best way we have to navigate through unpredictable, unfamiliar, and complex territory, because it makes us more adaptive and creative in the face of uncertainty. You may view scientific thinking as something reserved for professional scientists, but it's actually a life skill for all of us. Practicing scientific thinking the way it is illustrated in this book puts you on a journey of integrating it into your organization's culture and answers questions such as:

- How do you align your organization so that, through their individual and team goals, everyone is ultimately working toward shared customer-oriented objectives?

- How do you make innovative improvement happen at every level?

- How do you ensure that each team works toward its goals in a systematic, scientific way, rather than jumping to conclusions?

Aligning an organization so everyone in it is working toward common goals has been an elusive goal in the business world. There have been many mechanical attempts to achieve this by "cascading" targets and metrics into an organization, but today we realize that we should, in tandem, develop the planning and execution skills of the people in the organization. We know, too, that building those skills takes practice, often starting with some simple practice routines, or "Starter Kata."

Nowadays we often work in teams across departments, so ideally we have a shared set of skills that allow us to quickly and effectively work together. Scientific thinking is that kind of teamwork-enabling skill, and practicing it is at the root of building adaptive capability and culture. This book and its companions, *Toyota Kata* and *The Toyota Kata Practice Guide*,[1] focus on the people-development aspect of Toyota's management system. At Toyota the management hierarchy is responsible for improvement, and it uses daily work as the setting for practicing scientific thinking skills, with managers providing the coaching. The Improvement Kata and Coaching Kata make the fundamentals of that process transferrable beyond Toyota to any organization.

Practicing the Improvement Kata and Coaching Kata doesn't supplant your current improvement methods. It helps build foundational skills that make you better at whatever improvement methods you use. What we especially like about practicing the Improvement Kata and Coaching Kata is that they give us a way to be creative, to communicate about issues without accusation, to become engaged, to think differently, and to test and fail with learning, not repercussions. However, the Kata themselves are not the goal. They are a means to an end: a set of practice routines for creating something bigger.

Learning Organizations

A "learning organization" gains knowledge through experience and experiment as a regular part of its everyday activities. It's about building a decentralized, objective-driven management system that utilizes brainpower at each level, creating an agile whole that thrives in complex, dynamic conditions by improving, adapting, and innovating.

The learning organization concept has been around since 1978,[2] but surprisingly few organizations have been able to operationalize it. One reason is that being a learning organization involves some scientific thinking habits that do not come naturally to us, such as:

- Improving in a strategic direction, rather than making random efficiency improvements.

- Systematically observing and measuring simply to understand.

- Defining specific future conditions predicted to lead to desired outcomes.

---

1 Publication in Fall 2017

2 Argyris, Chris, and Donald A. Schön, *Organizational Learning: A Theory of Action Perspective*, Boston: Addison Wesley, 1978.

- Going beyond implementation to experimentation.

- Making specific predictions in order to enable learning and adjusting.

The practice routines of the Improvement Kata and Coaching Kata give you basic building blocks for creating your own learning organization. Almost any organization can scale up toward thinking and working scientifically, via the kind of coached practice we have tried to clearly illustrate here.

Value Stream Mapping

This book also helps ensure that the popular Value Stream Mapping (VSM) tool gets used in its intended role. VSM is a method for analyzing the current state and designing a future state for the series of events that take a product or service from its beginning through to the customer. The main purpose of Value Stream Mapping is to give a sense of direction.[3]

Many VSM training materials have suggested drawing "kaizen lightning bursts" on the current-state map, to highlight sources of waste and other opportunities. This is incorrect. Do *not* put kaizen lightning bursts on a current-state map, because a "go find stuff to improve" approach leads to random, unaligned, and unscientific efforts. The reason for drawing a current-state map is not to see problems, waste, or improvement opportunities for quick resolution, but to provide a basis for designing a future-state value stream.

Once you understand the current state, draw a future-state map of how you would like the value stream to function, for its customers, six months to three years from now. *Then* add lightning bursts to that future-state map, to highlight the construction sites you think will be necessary for achieving your desired future state. It's the future-state map that helps you focus and align individual improvement efforts by aiming them at an overarching goal. In the pages that follow notice how our example company, Acme Gearbox, utilizes VSM to help establish a strategic challenge and then utilizes the skills taught by practicing the Improvement Kata and Coaching Kata to work toward that challenge.

Over to You

We never know exactly what steps will lead to our goals, but we can practice and learn how to reach goals. Ideally, scientific thinking capabilities will be spread throughout an

---

3 One of us, Mike, is co-author of the original guidebook that introduced VSM.

organization, which makes teaching them the responsibility of every manager. In fact, today the routines of the Improvement Kata and Coaching Kata are being practiced in organizations in just about every imaginable industry.

Organizational culture can be seen as *mindset imparted by our experiences at work*. We've been watching the development of a more scientific thinking mindset at organizations that practice and experiment with chains of Kata coaching up and down their organization. It works remarkably well. Let us paint the picture for you.

Mike Rother	and	Gerd Aulinger
Ann Arbor, Michigan		Munich, Germany
January 2017		

INTRODUCTION

LET'S PAINT A PICTURE

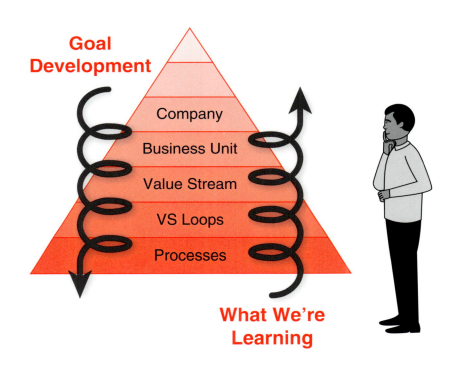

Making an Aligned Organization a Reality

This book paints a picture of how you can turn strategy and execution into everyday activity at all levels. The Improvement Kata and Coaching Kata are about practicing routines of goal-oriented creativity so they become habitual and help you build a deliberate, scientific thinking culture. As teams inside an organization pursue their individual goals, they are united by an overarching strategic challenge *and* a scientific way of thinking and working.

This is some of the essence of what the Lean community calls "policy deployment," "policy management," "hoshin kanri," or "strategy deployment."

An organization that is able to achieve challenging goals

Our goal is not to show you precisely how your policy deployment system should look and function. That's impossible because each organization has unique characteristics and exists in unique conditions. Developing an organization's managerial system is not about copying the tools and techniques that another organization has come up with, which would be jumping to solutions.

However, you can and should start with some common basics and then expand upon them through your own iterative process of trial and adjustment. The goals of this workbook are to show you what a working policy deployment system looks like and how to start building your own by practicing a set of fundamental routines, or *Starter Kata*.

With this book we intend to illustrate how to create a *living* organizational system that adapts, innovates, and continuously improves. The essence of policy deployment is not so complicated, but it takes practice and time to develop enough people with Improvement Kata and Coaching Kata skills to comprise an effective, interconnected chain of coaching dialogues, as we depict in this book. Think of the picture that this book paints as a goal to iteratively work toward.

There is more to learn and we will, of course, miss things that will be important for you. But if you are willing to practice and adjust, this book gives you enough of a map to enable you to work to develop a system that suits your organization and situation.

Scientific Thinking

Scientific thinking is a routine of intentional coordination between what we predict will happen next, seeing what actually happens, and adjusting based on what we learn from the difference. At the core of scientific thinking is curiosity about a world we will never understand fully but we might take the next step to understand a little better. You can utilize scientific thinking throughout your organization to help you achieve all sorts of challenging goals, navigating from here to there along unpredictable paths.

The basic pattern of scientific thinking

The Typical Progression of Skill Acquisition

As nice as it would be, you can't "implement" the picture we paint in this book. Skills and behaviors are internalized in our brain's automatic systems as a sort of habit. Modifying these automatic systems takes practice via actual activity. You modify an organizational culture by deliberately getting enough people in the organization to act differently. New thinking grows and eventually replaces the old.

The picture of an aligned and learning organization that we paint in this book represents a pretty high level of scientific thinking skill, especially among middle managers who are, by default, the day-to-day teachers in an organization. Any organization that wants to adopt policy deployment faces a skills and behavior progression that looks something like this:

3—Able to TEACH scientific improvement thinking as a *coach*

2—Able to APPLY scientific improvement thinking as a *learner*

1—AWARE of the pattern of scientific improvement thinking

What this means is that those critical middle managers should first become competent in the pattern of good improvement thinking by practicing it themselves, before they coach others. This should give you a sense for the task the organization faces. Culture modification is a challenging goal.

Making policy deployment work involves developing new thinking patterns. Practicing the routines of the Improvement Kata and Coaching Kata is a way of helping you learn those thinking patterns.

What Are Kata? They're About Learning with the Body[1]

Here are two different definitions for the word *Kata*. We'll use both:

- A **way of doing something**; an overall pattern.

- A small, **structured practice routine**. Learning and then combining these individual practice routines is a way of developing competency in the overall *way* or pattern of doing something.

Kata are structured routines that get practiced deliberately, especially at the beginning, so their pattern becomes a habit and leaves you with new abilities. Practicing Kata is a way of learning fundamental skill elements that you can combine and build on. The word comes from the martial arts where Kata are used to train combatants in fundamental moves, but the idea of practicing Kata can be applied in a much broader sense. This book is about deploying the practice routines of the Improvement Kata and Coaching Kata, which are ways of training people in a practical, universal pattern of scientific thinking.

At first you try to practice each Kata exactly as described, until it becomes somewhat automatic and habitual for you. That can take several weeks of practice. When you have

---

1 We are indebted to our colleague, Pierre Nadeau, for the phrase, "Learning with the body."

learned through practice to understand the "why" behind a Kata's routine, then you can start to deviate from it by evolving your own version or style—as long as its core principles remain intact.

This book utilizes a well-proven set of Starter Kata to practice every day. They come from the Toyota Kata research findings[2] and have been put into practice at organizations around the world.

The Improvement Kata and Coaching Kata

As shown in the illustration below, the Improvement Kata (IK) is a four-step **model or pattern of scientific thinking and working**. It's a *meta skill* that's useful at every level of an

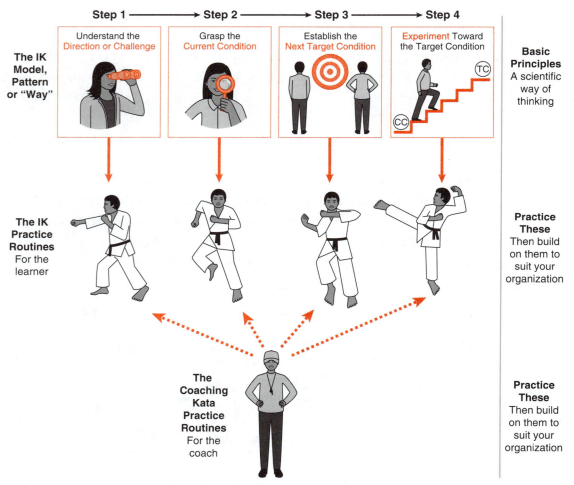

The practice routines of the Improvement Kata and Coaching Kata are starter drills for developing a scientific way of thinking.

2 For more information see the book *Toyota Kata* (2009) and visit the Toyota Kata website.

organization. Importantly, each step of the Improvement Kata model also includes **simple, structured practice routines**, i.e., Starter Kata. In this book we illustrate how those routines get practiced throughout an organization, as a way of learning how to think and work scientifically when you are pursuing goals as a team.

The Coaching Kata, in turn, is a **practice routine for teaching the Improvement Kata pattern**.

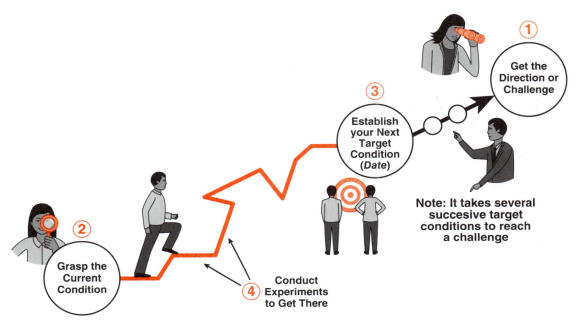

Here's one way to envision the four steps of the Improvement Kata pattern.

The Improvement Kata Has Two Phases

As shown in the diagram below, the Improvement Kata model has a *planning* phase and an *executing* phase.

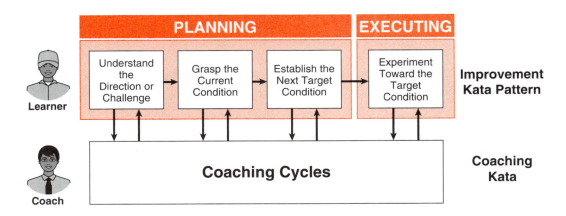

In step one of the Improvement Kata pattern, the challenge or direction comes from one level above the learner. The remaining three steps are then undertaken by the learner at the learner's level. As the learner works, the coach or manager provides corrective inputs on the learner's *procedure*. For instance, the learner's target condition (step three of the Improvement Kata) is not provided by their manager or coach, but is developed by the learner in dialogue with the coach. The coach provides daily procedural feedback to get the learner's target condition to be appropriate and well developed; not taking over the effort but rather helping the learner practice the process.

Planning Phase
Consensus on direction and specific focal points is developed. Target conditions and coaching topics are established mathematically and in detail down through the organization's levels. At their processes, learners work to grasp the current condition and establish their next target condition. Daily coaching cycles are scheduled.

Executing Phase
Once a learner has established their next target condition, a daily cycle of frequent experiments (also called "PDCA cycles"), coaching cycles, and upward communication of the evolving current condition and lessons-learned begins.

The coach gives mostly procedural inputs, yet is also responsible for the quality of the learner's work. This overlap creates a connection between the learner and the coach. The learner is the coach's resource for getting things done, but the coach doesn't tell the learner what to do, since no one can know in advance exactly how to reach the next target condition. Instead, managers in this system guide people into finding their own answers scientifically through experimentation. The manager focuses on having the learner practice good scientific procedure.

As you can see, it's important to realize that the process of policy deployment is not a simple downward cascade of goals from above which many people may envision. Rather, it is a back and forth process between coaches and their learners, which cuts across each level of the organization. This process takes practice and time to set up, carry out, and master. The core skillsets are what you learn by practicing the Improvement Kata and Coaching Kata.

A Simple Case Example: Acme Gearbox Company

To illustrate the chain of Kata coaching, we'll use a simplified example of a gearbox manufacturing value stream (VS), which has three successive processes as shown below. Try to keep in mind that technical details of the gearbox example itself are not the point. We're using this manufacturing example because of its high volume and easy visibility, but the practice routines we illustrate suit nearly any type and size of organization. *The details of those routines are the point.*

Process one is **gear machining**, which involves several processing steps (cutting, broaching, etc.) and groups of machines to carry out those steps. This is followed by **assembly,** where the gears are attached to shafts and gearboxes are completed with components, including electronics, gear-shift mechanisms, and oil. After testing in assembly, the gearbox is sent to **shipping,** where it gets packed in a crate and sent to the customer.

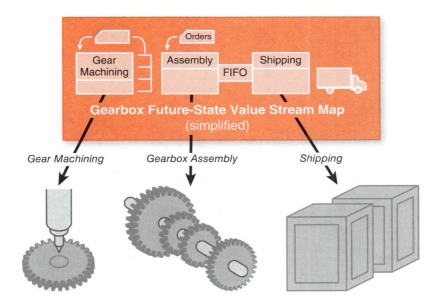

The gearbox production value stream has three process loops.

Meet the Five Main Players in the Gearbox Value Stream

To illustrate the roles at each level of the organization, we'll look at one vertical slice of Acme's hierarchical pyramid. Although you see just one person per level, please envision each person as the manager of a team below them, and also having several colleagues at their own level. (We discuss coaching horizontally in Chapter 4.)

You'll notice that although the scope of improvement efforts differs from level to level, the patterns of the Improvement Kata and Coaching Kata are content-neutral and get repeated at each level.

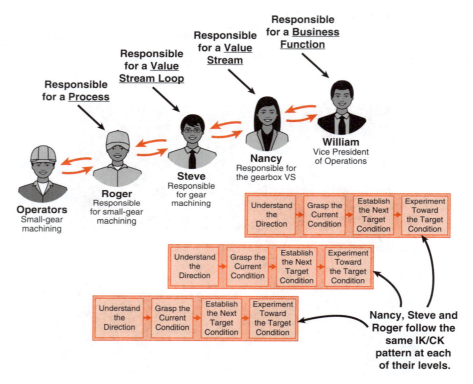

Each level follows the same IK/CK pattern.

	Aware	Able to DO	Able to TEACH
Senior Managers	●	●	●
Middle Managers	●	●	◑
Process Level	●	◑	○

Current Improvement Kata/Coaching Kata skill levels at ACME

The Coach/Learner Pairing Repeats Across Each Level

At each level in our picture, every organization member has a next-level-up coach. Likewise, in the opposite direction each person has a group of learners. So the roles of learner and coach are fractal, interlinking all members of the organization with a common language, structure, and way of working. A *fractal* is something that has the same or a similar pattern at each scale level.

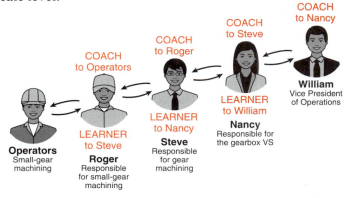

Coach/Learner pairings

There Are Three Main Roles in Improvement Kata Practice

1. **LEARNER (or mentee):** This person is responsible for the doing. The learner applies the Improvement Kata pattern and practice routines at the level and process for which they are responsible. The learner knows the challenge, grasps the current condition at their process, establishes the next target condition for that process, and works toward it by conducting experiments (to develop solutions) against the obstacles they encounter. This is done in dialogue with the coach through daily "coaching cycles."

2. **COACH (or mentor):** This person is responsible for teaching scientific thinking skills and for the learner's results. The coach ensures that the learner is working scientifically according to the Improvement Kata pattern. He or she conducts the daily coaching cycles, which are guided by the Starter Kata pattern of the five Coaching Kata questions. The coach's job is to develop the learner by providing corrective feedback to the learner on Improvement Kata procedure, not to improve the process themselves.

3. **SECOND COACH (not illustrated above):** This person is responsible for the coach's coaching. The second coach periodically observes coaching cycles between the coach and learner and gives feedback to the coach to help the coach grow their coaching skills. This "coach the coach" role may be filled by a person one level up from the coach, by a peer of the coach, or by a staff specialist.

Each Learner Has a Storyboard That Looks like This

The Learner's Storyboard Follows the Pattern in the Coaching Cycles

The learner's storyboard is utilized in the daily coaching cycles to support the dialogue between the learner and the coach. The board's layout follows the pattern of the coaching conversation, starting at the left and finishing with the reflection and next step on the right side. Forms and data corresponding to the Starter Kata are posted on the storyboard (which itself is a Starter Kata) as shown.

As with any Starter Kata that you practice, eventually your organization's storyboard design can evolve to suit the characteristics of your environment and culture.

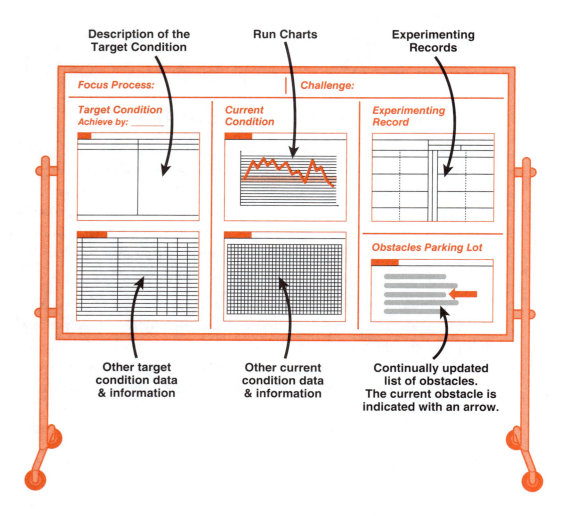

Start with this storyboard format.

Each Coach Has a Five-Question Card That Looks like This

The five Coaching Kata questions are another Starter Kata. They are the framework for the daily coaching cycles between the learner and the coach. The five questions reinforce the pattern of the Improvement Kata and help the coach see how the learner is currently thinking.

As with practicing any Kata, eventually your organization's coaching questions can evolve to suit the characteristics of your environment and culture, as long as the fundamental pattern and principles of the five-question Starter Kata remains.

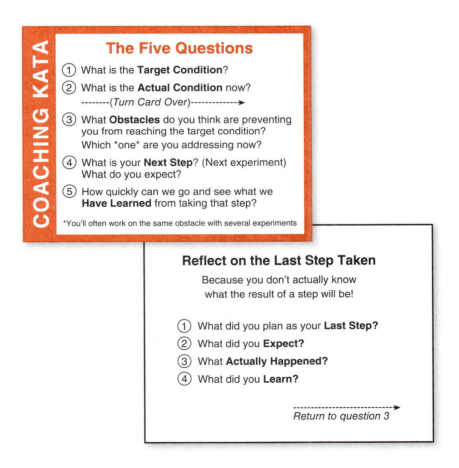

Start with this set of coaching questions and then build on them.

The Layout of This Book

The book layout has two sides in two colors:

- The **white right-side pages** contain the main story, told through coaching cycle dialogues.

- The **color shaded left-side pages** provide background information, such as illustrating the forms being used in the coaching cycles.

Occasionally we will interrupt the story with **lined two-page spreads** to clarify key points. You'll recognize these pages by their "notebook paper" background.

As you go through the book, read the story on the right side. There you'll find the chain of Kata coaching dialogues that's such a vital ingredient of a true up and down policy deployment system. But one word of caution: try to pay attention to the details of the Acme story so you can see how the connections work. Again, the fact that Acme is a manufacturing company is beside the point.

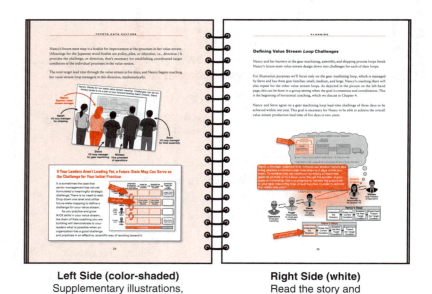

Left Side (color-shaded)
Supplementary illustrations,
forms, and explanations

Right Side (white)
Read the story and
corresponding coaching
dialogues here

The left-page, right-page layout of this book.

Before We Get Started:
Why Build a Management System like This?

The teaching practices and resulting entrepreneurial skillset described in this book are well-suited for confronting challenges and successfully navigating the unpredictable path between here and there. The organization, in essence, works to develop a content-neutral scientific thinking capability—a *meta skill*—into which it can introduce nearly any challenge. The stronger and more widespread the organization's scientific thinking capability—its culture—the bigger the challenges it can take on.

Your organization has power when it can combine setting tough challenges with teams that have mastered an effective way of meeting such challenges.

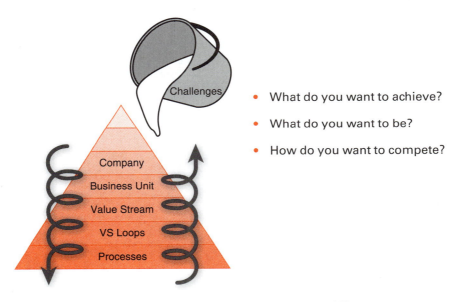

- What do you want to achieve?
- What do you want to be?
- How do you want to compete?

With increasing scientific thinking skill comes the ability to introduce and handle almost any challenge.

Policy deployment is not really the mechanical system of establishing a chain of linked goals, as has often been depicted in the Lean community, but more broadly an ongoing system of management that develops creative capability while applying it to tough goals; to help ensure the organization's success and survival in the long run.

You may already be practicing the Improvement Kata pattern with a coach, or perhaps you are coaching. With that, you are practicing the core fractal, or "playing the violin" so to speak. But you are also part of an organization, which is like an orchestra. The goal is not just to play the violin, but to *make music as a group*. Toward that end, this book shows you how to *conduct an orchestra*.

CHAPTER 1

PLANNING

Understand the Challenge,
Grasp the Current Condition,
Establish the Next Target Condition

About the Planning Phase Chapter

Going a Little Slower to Then Be Focused and Fast

When we are faced with a tough goal we have a natural tendency to jump right into action. After all, the sooner we get going, the sooner we'll get there, right?

Not necessarily.

We often don't view planning as *action*, and thus we end up getting poor results because, in our zeal to get going, we jump to conclusions and start "implementing" preconceived ideas too quickly. Don't be offended, we do it too. It's a natural tendency of our brain, which quickly fills in missing information without alerting us that it is doing so.

The planning phase of the Improvement Kata pattern involves these three steps:

1. Getting some clarity about the challenge that's coming from above, and what it means for your level.

2. Digging deep into your level or focus process, with facts and data, to better understand its current condition.

3. Establishing your next target condition (TK), based on the current condition (CC) and in the direction of the challenge.

This planning prepares you to move more effectively into the zone of uncertainty of the executing phase, where we apply our creativity by viewing each step toward the next target condition as an experiment, from which we will learn something.

"Wouldn't it be great if we could . . . "

ACME'S CHALLENGE

Your Gearbox
Your Way
One Week

As You Might Expect, Our Story Starts with the Customer at the *Organization* Level

Creating and Providing Strategic Direction for the Organization

The strategy deployment process begins at the top of the organization, with leadership's intention of better serving customers in a way that differentiates your organization's offerings in the marketplace. This should be an aspirational challenge that sets a future vision to strive for. Think of completing the sentence, *"Wouldn't it be great if we could . . ."*

Acme's senior managers have done a thorough analysis and learned that Acme can distinguish itself with customers by increasing its product variety while simultaneously reducing the lead time required to get a gearbox to the customer.

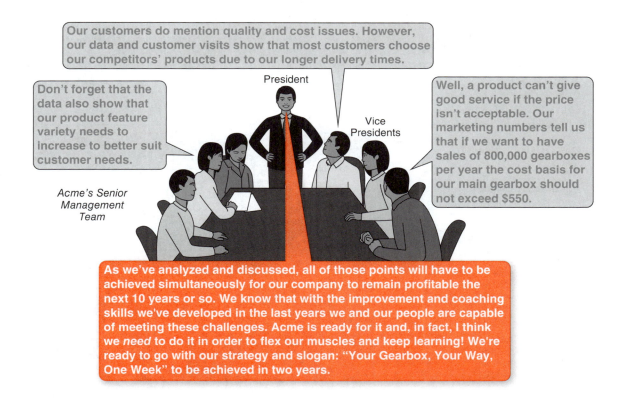

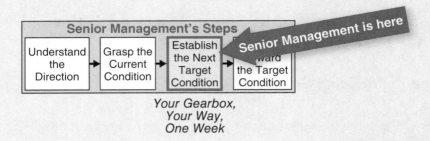

Senior Management's Steps

| Understand the Direction | Grasp the Current Condition | Establish the Next Target Condition | ...ward the Target Condition |

Senior Management is here

Your Gearbox,
Your Way,
One Week

Acme's senior management has been establishing a target condition for the organization level, which at that level equals *strategy*. Note that there are specific calculations behind the strategy deliberations. As we will see, these numbers are then used by product (value stream) managers to calculate and define a target condition for each product family's value stream.

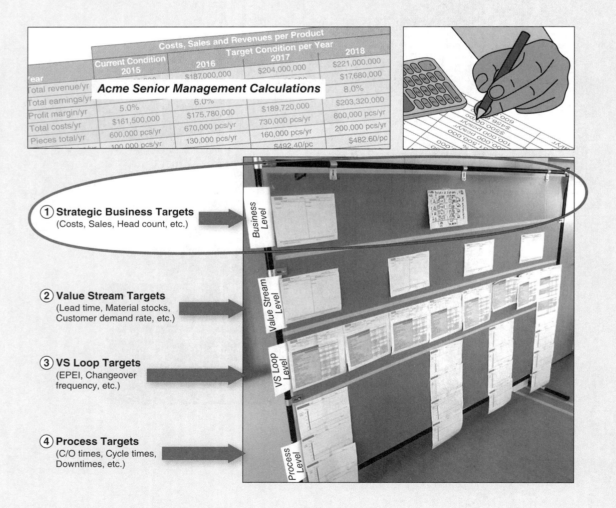

Acme Senior Management Calculations

Costs, Sales and Revenues per Product			
	Current Condition 2015	Target Condition per Year	
Year		2016	2017	2018
Total revenue/yr		$187,000,000	$204,000,000	$221,000,000
Total earnings/yr				$17,680,000
Profit margin/yr	5.0%	6.0%		8.0%
Total costs/yr	$161,500,000	$175,780,000	$189,720,000	$203,320,000
Pieces total/yr	600,000 pcs/yr	670,000 pcs/yr	730,000 pcs/yr	800,000 pcs/yr
	100,000 pcs/yr	130,000 pcs/yr	160,000 pcs/yr	200,000 pcs/yr
			$492.40/pc	$482.60/pc

① **Strategic Business Targets**
(Costs, Sales, Head count, etc.)

Business Level

② **Value Stream Targets**
(Lead time, Material stocks, Customer demand rate, etc.)

Value Stream Level

③ **VS Loop Targets**
(EPEI, Changeover frequency, etc.)

VS Loop Level

④ **Process Targets**
(C/O times, Cycle times, Downtimes, etc.)

Process Level

Sharing the Strategic Direction and Purpose with the *Value Stream* Level

After having agreed at the senior management level about the strategic direction to strive for in the next two years, **William,** the vice president of operations, and his executive colleagues each enter a dialogue with their direct reports about the challenge and its purpose.

William starts by explaining to Nancy, owner of Acme's gearbox value stream (and one of William's learners), the reasons for the **current direction of the company** and the purpose of the company's strategy for serving its customers even better. William explains that the gearbox business is increasingly becoming a make-to-order business. Acme can realize a competitive advantage if its lead time to the customer can be **five days** for any gearbox configuration with features the customer wants, built from a range of modular standard gears, at target cost. This is the senior-level target condition for meeting the overall challenge, or theme, that Acme leadership is calling, **"Your Gearbox, Your Way, One Week."**

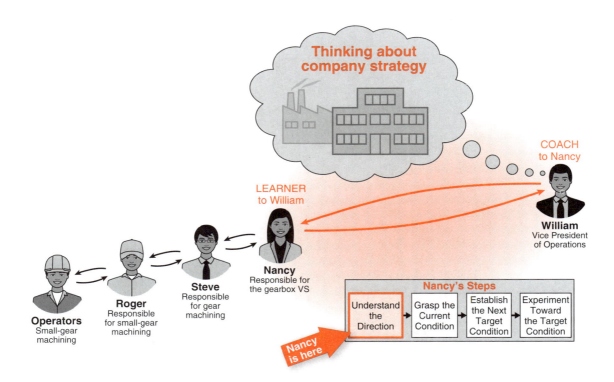

The Role of Leadership

In the case of senior management, coaching others is not enough. Illustrated below are typical responsibilities for an organization's leaders. In short, the leaders should have a clear picture of where the organization wants to go, be able to communicate that, and ensure that the organization practices the skills for meeting such challenges.

1. Understand customers, potential customers, markets, and environments in which the organization operates. Recognize what it is that customers need.

2. Establish direction. Develop strategies to meet customer needs in a way that differentiates the organization from its competitors.

3. Ensure effective execution by having managers develop their people's problem-solving capabilities as they strive to achieve goals in line with the strategic concept.

4. Continually assess the impact of strategy and adjust as necessary.

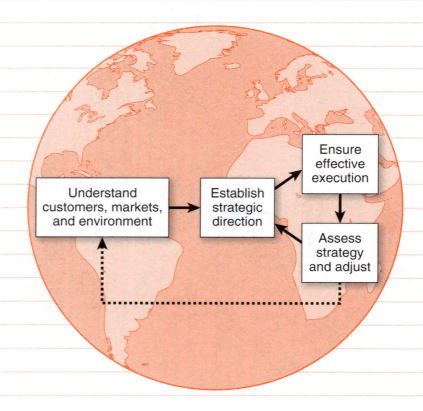

The Role of a Challenge. What Do We *Need* to Do?

A *vision* is a long-range ideal, stated by the organization's leadership, of value flowed to the customer. However, for day-to-day work and improvement activity, an even more important way to give direction is a closer and more specific *challenge*. A *challenge* is a measureable description of success 1–3 years in the future. The challenge is where strategy and execution meet.

Having an organization- or value stream–level challenge is important, so each learner's individual target condition is seen as connected and meaningful. It's difficult for people to stay engaged with something that doesn't have a purpose.

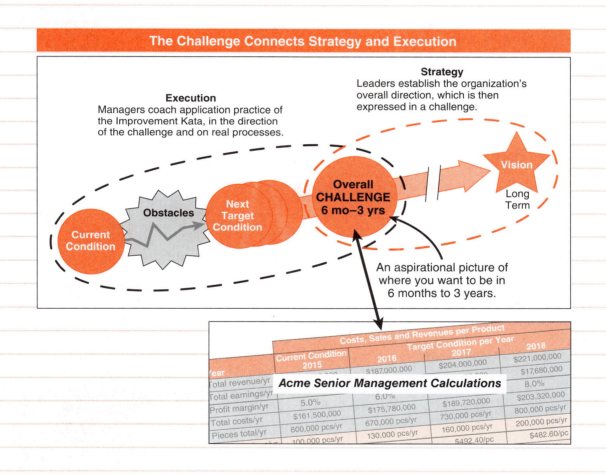

Source: The Toyota Kata Practice Guide

The Overall Challenge Gets Deployed

The process of breaking down the overall challenge into connected challenges at each level is done through the coach/learner dialogues that cut across the levels. In many cases the target condition from the level above becomes the challenge for the next level down.

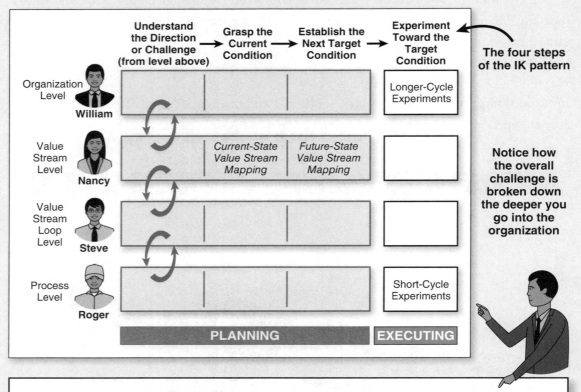

Value Stream Mapping Helps You Define and Communicate a Direction

Value Stream Mapping (VSM) is a method for analyzing the current state and designing a future state for the series of events that take a product or service from its beginning through to the customer.

Think of a future-state value stream map as a challenge that focuses and aims individual improvement efforts toward a shared breakthrough goal. The future-state map defines the common direction for improvement at the individual processes inside the value stream, which helps to connect the process improvement efforts in each area. A future-state value stream map is sometimes even called a *challenge map*.

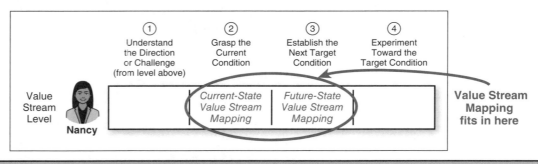

Nancy

Next Level Down:
Nancy Works at the *Value Stream* Level

Understanding the Current Value Stream and Establishing a Target Value Stream Design

One level down, **Nancy**, manager of the gearbox product family, takes William's five-day production lead time target condition as her challenge, and works to translate it into a target condition for her value stream. Nancy analyzes and maps the current state of the gearbox value stream. Then, based on the strategic direction she received from William, *she designs a future state for this value stream* to be achieved within the two-year time frame of the company challenge. This future-state value stream design is the core of Nancy's target condition.

Nancy is drawing her ideas about what her value stream would have to be like in order to meet the five-day lead time challenge. Much is still to be learned, and Nancy will keep fine tuning her value stream design as her direct reports move forward and learn more through their experiments.

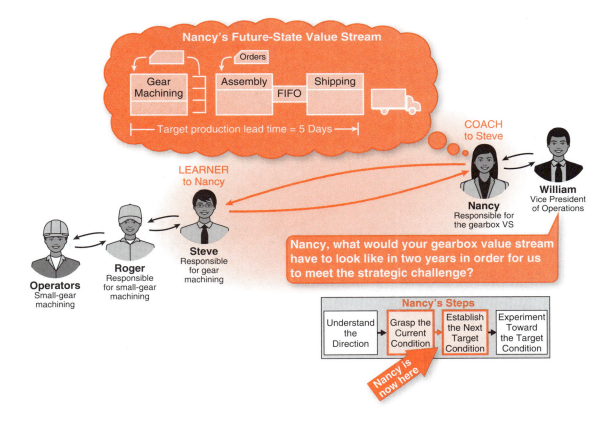

Nancy's future-state map is a hoshin for improvement at the processes in her value stream. (Meanings for the Japanese word *hoshin* are *policy*, *plan*, or *objective*, i.e., *direction*.) It provides the challenge, or direction, that's necessary for establishing coordinated target conditions at the individual processes in the value stream.

The total target lead time through the value stream is five days, and Nancy begins coaching her value stream loop managers in this direction, mathematically.

If Your Leaders Aren't Leading Yet, a Future-State Map Can Serve as the Challenge for Your Initial Practice

It is sometimes the case that senior management has not yet formulated a meaningful strategic challenge. There is no need to wait. Drop down one level and utilize future-state mapping to define a challenge for your value stream.

As you practice and grow IK/CK skills in your value stream, the chain of Kata coaching you are building will demonstrate to your leaders what is possible when an organization has a good challenge and practices an effective, scientific way of working toward it.

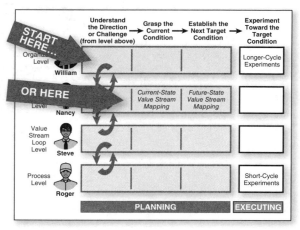

Defining Value Stream *Loop* Challenges

Nancy and her learners in the gear machining, assembly, and shipping process loops break Nancy's future-state value stream design down into challenges for each of their loops.

For illustration purposes we'll focus only on the gear machining loop, which is managed by Steve and has three gear families: small, medium, and large. Nancy's coaching there will also repeat for the other value stream loops. As depicted in the picture on the left-hand page, this can be done in a group setting when the goal is consensus and coordination. This is the beginning of horizontal coaching, which we discuss in Chapter 4.

Nancy and Steve agree on a gear machining loop lead-time challenge of three days to be achieved within one year. This goal is necessary for Nancy to be able to achieve the overall value stream production lead time of five days in two years.

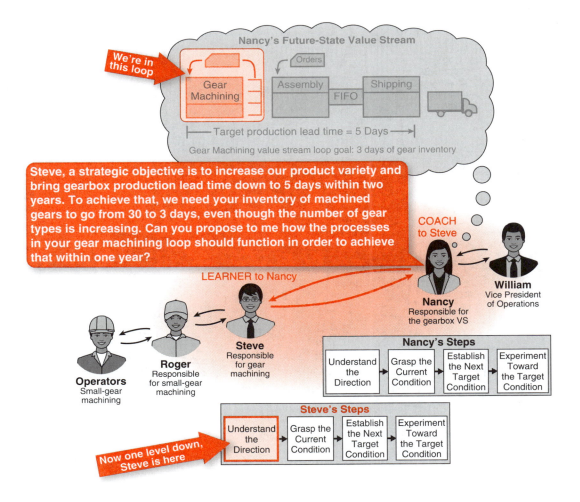

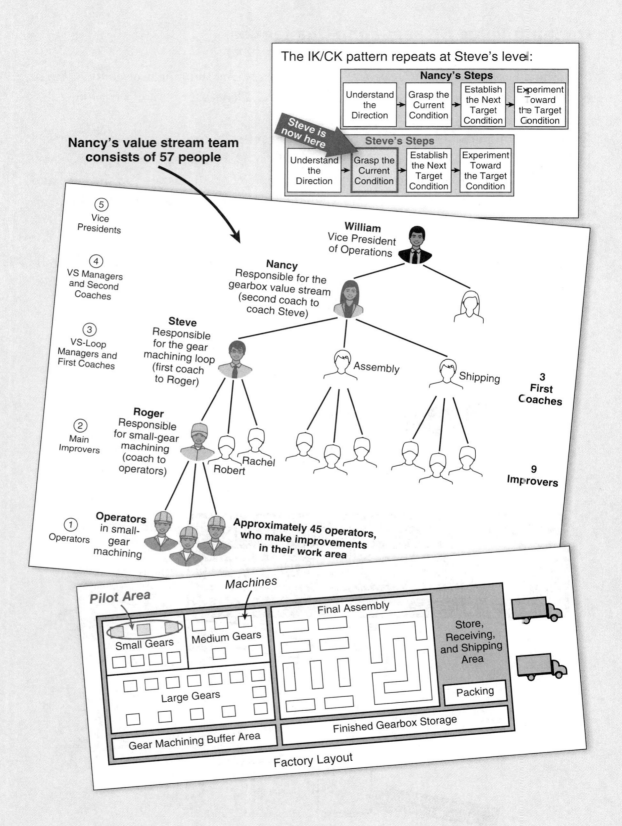

The IK/CK pattern repeats at Steve's level:

Nancy's Steps

Understand the Direction → Grasp the Current Condition → Establish the Next Target Condition → Experiment Toward the Target Condition

Steve is now here →

Steve's Steps

Understand the Direction → Grasp the Current Condition → Establish the Next Target Condition → Experiment Toward the Target Condition

Nancy's value stream team consists of 57 people

⑤ Vice Presidents

④ VS Managers and Second Coaches

③ VS-Loop Managers and First Coaches

② Main Improvers

① Operators

William Vice President of Operations

Nancy Responsible for the gearbox value stream (second coach to coach Steve)

Steve Responsible for the gear machining loop (first coach to Roger)

Assembly

Shipping

3 First Coaches

Roger Responsible for small-gear machining (coach to operators)

Robert

Rachel

9 Improvers

Operators in small-gear machining

Approximately 45 operators, who make improvements in their work area

Pilot Area

Machines

Small Gears

Medium Gears

Final Assembly

Store, Receiving, and Shipping Area

Large Gears

Packing

Gear Machining Buffer Area

Finished Gearbox Storage

Factory Layout

Steve

Next Level Down:
Steve Works at the Value Stream *Loop* Level

Steve decides to begin with a pilot effort within the small-gear machining area of his value stream loop, which is supervised by Roger. Steve has three supervisors in gear machining: Roger (small gears), Rachel (medium gears), and Robert (large gears). Steve decides to engage all three supervisors in the small-gear machining pilot first, to give them some practice, and soon expand the activity to medium and large gears.

In our example we will focus only on Roger. The approach Steve applies with Roger will also be applied with Rachel and Robert, who will also have daily coaching cycles with Steve.

Steve now has to grasp the current condition in small-gear machining.

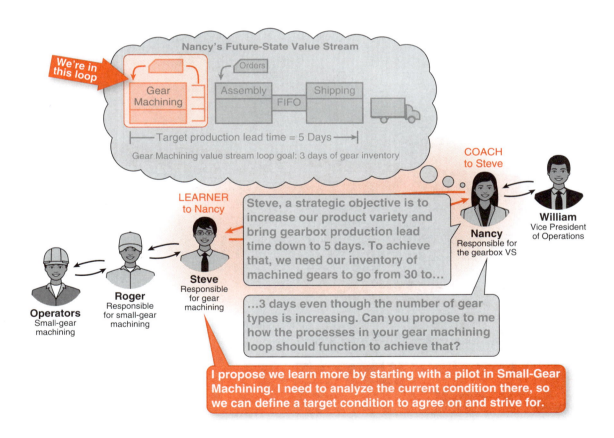

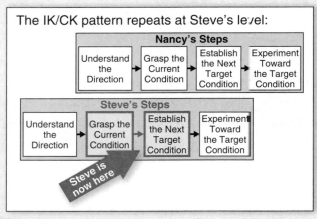

The IK/CK pattern repeats at Steve's level:

Nancy's Steps
Understand the Direction → Grasp the Current Condition → Establish the Next Target Condition → Experiment Toward the Target Condition

Steve's Steps
Understand the Direction → Grasp the Current Condition → Establish the Next Target Condition → Experiment Toward the Target Condition

Steve is now here

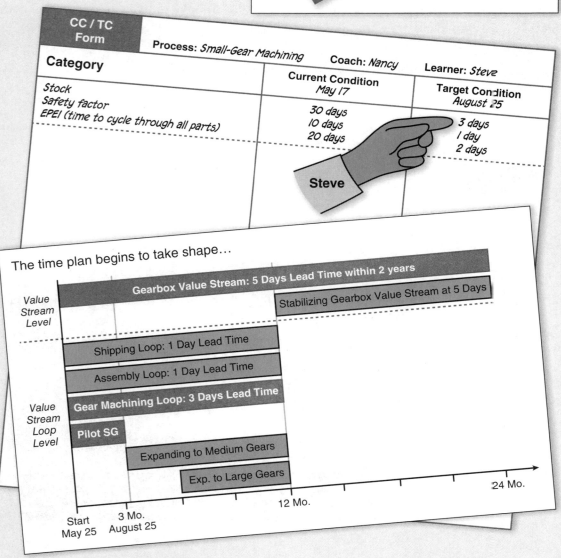

CC / TC Form

Process: *Small-Gear Machining*   Coach: *Nancy*   Learner: *Steve*

Category	Current Condition May 17	Target Condition August 25
Stock	30 days	3 days
Safety factor	10 days	1 day
EPEI (time to cycle through all parts)	20 days	2 days

Steve

The time plan begins to take shape…

Value Stream Level
- Gearbox Value Stream: 5 Days Lead Time within 2 years
- Stabilizing Gearbox Value Stream at 5 Days

Value Stream Loop Level
- Shipping Loop: 1 Day Lead Time
- Assembly Loop: 1 Day Lead Time
- Gear Machining Loop: 3 Days Lead Time
- Pilot SG
- Expanding to Medium Gears
- Exp. to Large Gears

Start May 25   3 Mo. August 25   12 Mo.   24 Mo.

After analyzing the current condition in small-gear machining, learner Steve, guided by his coach, Nancy, starts to develop the next target condition on a current condition/target condition form, shown at left. This is done, in large part, mathematically. Nancy recommends giving the pilot a horizon of 90 days.

Steve's step-by-step calculations involve the EPEI (Every Part Every Interval) determination, which is explained on the next two pages.

Steve knows he has to reduce his stock from 30 days to a maximum of 3 days. He also knows that production does not always run smoothly every day, so he wants to maintain his current safety factor of 50 percent. In order to maintain one day of work-in-process inventory and meet the challenge, he'll have to cycle through all of the high-volume part types, plus some "specials," every 2 days, instead of every 20 days like he does now.

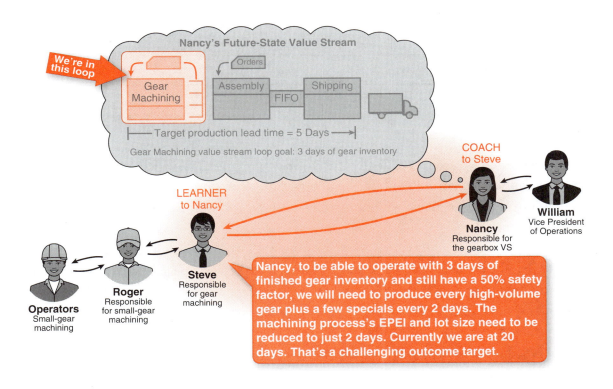

Steve's EPEI Calculation

Let's take a closer look at how Steve is calculating. Steve needs to go from the outcome target of three days of stock, to a *target condition* that describes how the small-gear machining loop should function in order for that outcome to be achieved. Steve has in mind Nancy's 90-day time frame for the pilot area target condition, which has an achieve-by date of August 25.

Nancy has asked Steve to propose to her a target condition that will allow him to produce 40 different gear types every 2 days, instead of 30 gear types in 20 days. This is a challenge at Steve's level, not unlike those that many managers may face at some point. But Steve does not jump to solutions. He instead starts to explore the variables he can influence and compares options by doing some EPEI math for the processes in his loop (EPEI = Every Part Every Interval).

$$\text{EPEI} = \frac{\text{Sum of the changeover times to produce all types}}{\text{Time available for changeovers per day}}$$

Since the product variety and lead time numbers are given, Steve has to work with the other variables he can influence at his loop's processes. For budget reasons, Steve also cannot invest in more machines, nor can he increase the 15 shifts per week working time.

The total number of item types is increasing from 30 to 40, which includes 12 "runners" that have to be made every 2 days, and 28 "specials." Of these specials Steve needs to allocate run time to make 4 of them every 2 days. That means, every 2 days, Steve's area will have to produce 16 different gears: 12 runners and 4 specials.

In the target condition, Steve's area will have to process 8 different gears every day, which means 8 changeovers. With current changeover times running between 70 and 90 minutes, it is clear this will require some significant changes in the way the small-gear machining loop operates.

Steve starts by looking at how much time he needs just to process the gears. He draws a bar to represent the 1,320 minutes of working time available each day. Based on current performance though, he loses about 20 percent of the total daily working time to downtime, which leaves 1,056 minutes to actually run the machines and perform the changeovers.

The small-gear shop needs to produce 12,120 pieces/month, or 606 pieces every day. Right now, it takes 120 seconds of run time for each gear. That means the gear shop needs 606 x 120 seconds = 1,212 minutes per day just to run the parts. That will not work, even if the changeover time were zero. There is too much downtime.

Steve thinks, "If we can reduce the unplanned downtime from 20 percent to 15 percent, that gives me 1,122 minutes of production time. That still isn't enough, but it's closer."

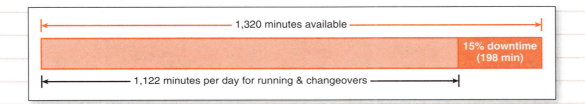

The current run time is 120 seconds per gear. "I know our manufacturing engineer is conservative, and I am pretty sure that time includes some minor stoppages. It also includes manual unload/load time, which I know we can improve. What if we can get the run time down to 100 seconds per gear? What do I have to work with then? 606 x 100 seconds = 1,010 minutes per day. OK, that's tight, but it fits.

"That leaves me 1,122 – 1,010 = 112 minutes to do 8 changeovers every day, which would get us through the 12 runners and 4 specials every 2 days. 112/8 = 14 minutes per changeover. Wow. That is going to be challenging, but I know that other companies have done this."

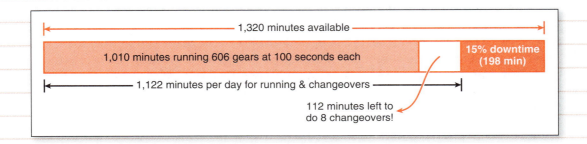

Steve summarized his calculations on a current condition/target condition form so he could share his thinking with Nancy in their next coaching cycle.

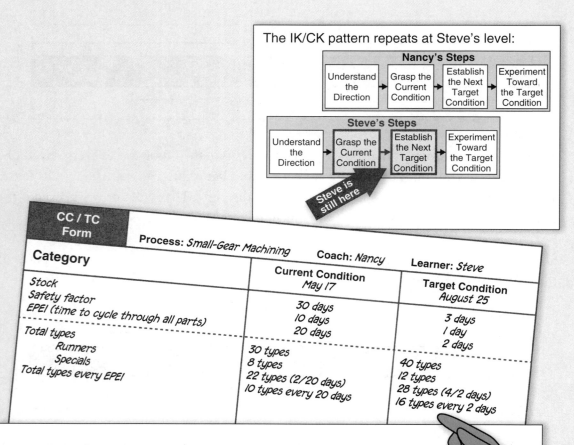

The IK/CK pattern repeats at Steve's level:

Nancy's Steps

| Understand the Direction | → | Grasp the Current Condition | → | Establish the Next Target Condition | → | Experiment Toward the Target Condition |

Steve's Steps

| Understand the Direction | → | Grasp the Current Condition | → | Establish the Next Target Condition | → | Experiment Toward the Target Condition |

Steve is still here

CC / TC Form

Process: *Small-Gear Machining*   Coach: *Nancy*   Learner: *Steve*

Category	Current Condition May 17	Target Condition August 25
Stock		
Safety factor	30 days	3 days
EPEI (time to cycle through all parts)	10 days	1 day
	20 days	2 days
Total types		
Runners	30 types	40 types
Specials	8 types	12 types
Total types every EPEI	22 types (2/20 days)	28 types (4/2 days)
	10 types every 20 days	16 types every 2 days

Steve

About the Current Condition/Target Condition Form: It's Another Starter Kata

The left-hand column of this form is for recording information about the current condition, and the right-hand column is for developing the target condition.

The left and right columns of this form, plus any additional pages of data such as block diagrams and run charts, are posted in the *current condition* and *target condition* fields of the learner's storyboard.

You may think that a target condition is a goal given to the learner by the coach, but that is incorrect. Developing the target condition is a back-and-forth process between the learner and the coach. The learner defines a target condition and proposes it to the coach. The learner receives feedback from the coach and fine-tunes the target condition accordingly. This process repeats until coach and learner come to consensus on the next target condition.

The coach asks the learner to use the right-hand column of the current condition/target condition form to describe how the learner would like the focus process to be operating on the achieve-by date. To do this the learner refers to the current condition summary in the left-hand column and answers the following questions as they fill out the right-hand column:

• Which process parameters do you want to keep the same?

• Which process parameters do you want to change?

In their next coaching cycle Steve walks Nancy through how he developed his proposed next target condition for the pilot in small-gear machining.

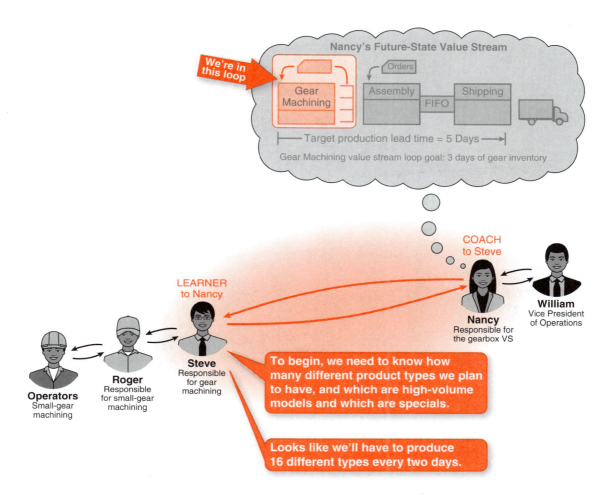

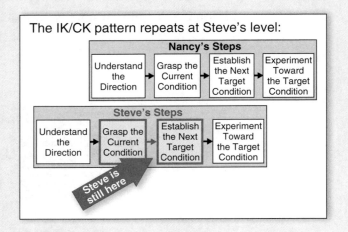

The IK/CK pattern repeats at Steve's level:

Nancy's Steps

Understand the Direction → Grasp the Current Condition → Establish the Next Target Condition → Experiment Toward the Target Condition

Steve's Steps

Understand the Direction → Grasp the Current Condition → Establish the Next Target Condition → Experiment Toward the Target Condition

Steve is still here

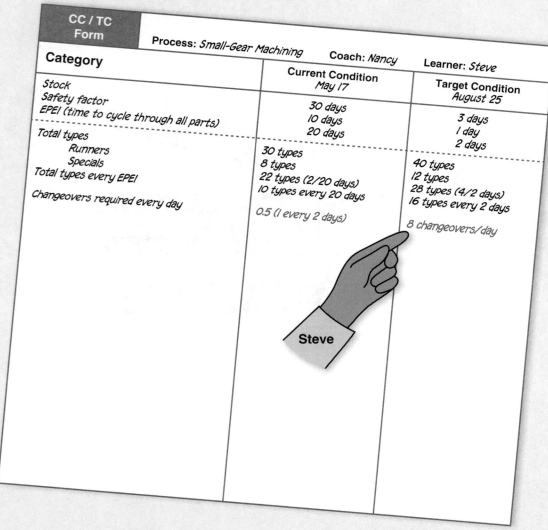

CC / TC Form

Process: *Small-Gear Machining* Coach: *Nancy* Learner: *Steve*

Category	Current Condition May 17	Target Condition August 25
Stock	30 days	3 days
Safety factor	10 days	1 day
EPEI (time to cycle through all parts)	20 days	2 days
Total types		
Runners	30 types	40 types
Specials	8 types	12 types
Total types every EPEI	22 types (2/20 days)	28 types (4/2 days)
	10 types every 20 days	16 types every 2 days
Changeovers required every day	0.5 (1 every 2 days)	8 changeovers/day

Steve

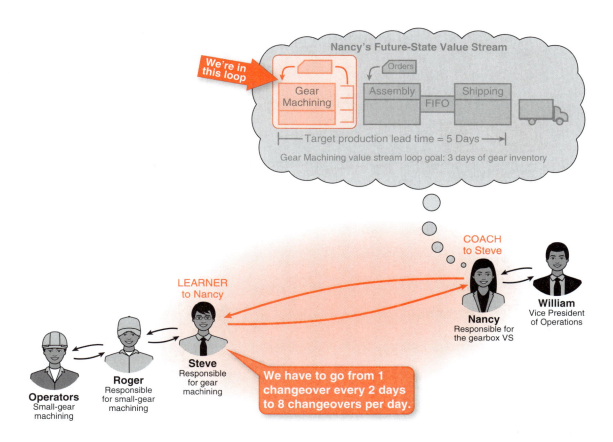

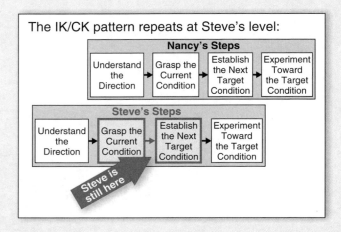

The IK/CK pattern repeats at Steve's level:

Nancy's Steps
Understand the Direction → Grasp the Current Condition → Establish the Next Target Condition → Experiment Toward the Target Condition

Steve's Steps
Understand the Direction → Grasp the Current Condition → Establish the Next Target Condition → Experiment Toward the Target Condition

Steve is still here

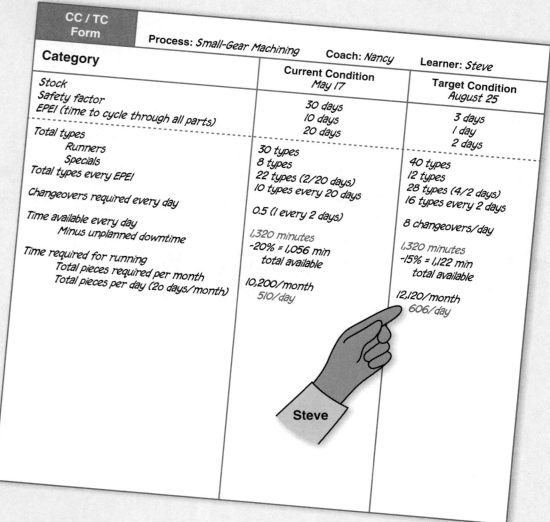

CC / TC Form

Process: *Small-Gear Machining*   Coach: *Nancy*   Learner: *Steve*

Category	Current Condition May 17	Target Condition August 25
Stock	30 days	3 days
Safety factor	10 days	1 day
EPEI (time to cycle through all parts)	20 days	2 days
Total types	30 types	40 types
Runners	8 types	12 types
Specials	22 types (2/20 days)	28 types (4/2 days)
Total types every EPEI	10 types every 20 days	16 types every 2 days
Changeovers required every day	0.5 (1 every 2 days)	8 changeovers/day
Time available every day	1,320 minutes	1,320 minutes
Minus unplanned downtime	-20% = 1,056 min total available	-15% = 1,122 min total available
Time required for running		
Total pieces required per month	10,200/month	12,120/month
Total pieces per day (20 days/month)	510/day	606/day

Steve

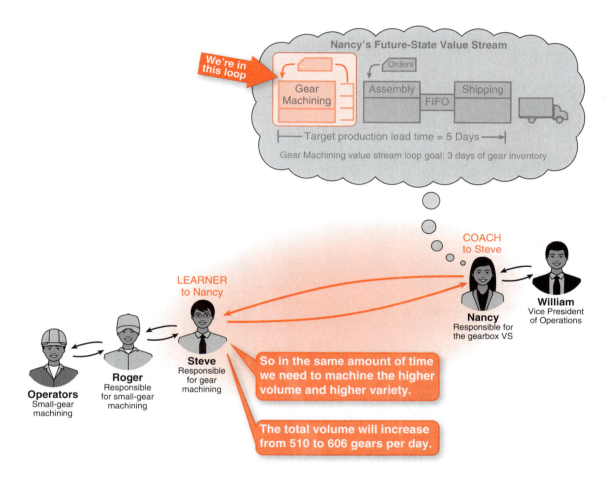

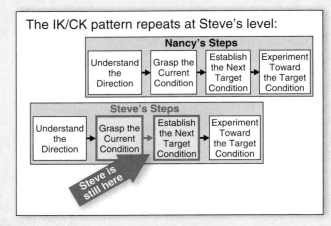

The IK/CK pattern repeats at Steve's level:

Nancy's Steps

Understand the Direction → Grasp the Current Condition → Establish the Next Target Condition → Experiment Toward the Target Condition

Steve's Steps

Understand the Direction → Grasp the Current Condition → Establish the Next Target Condition → Experiment Toward the Target Condition

Steve is still here

CC / TC Form

Process: *Small-Gear Machining*   Coach: *Nancy*   Learner: *Steve*

Category	Current Condition May 17	Target Condition August 25
Stock		
Safety factor	30 days	3 days
EPEI (time to cycle through all parts)	10 days	1 day
	20 days	2 days
Total types		
Runners	30 types	40 types
Specials	8 types	12 types
Total types every EPEI	22 types (2/20 days)	28 types (4/2 days)
	10 types every 20 days	16 types every 2 days
Changeovers required every day	0.5 (1 every 2 days)	8 changeovers/day
Time available every day	1,320 minutes	1,320 minutes
Minus unplanned downtime	-20% = 1,056 min total available	-15% = 1,122 min total available
Time required for running		
Total pieces required per month	10,200/month	12,120/month
Total pieces per day (20 days/month)	510/day	606/day
Planned run time (pl. cycle time)/item	120 seconds	100 seconds
Run time required/day (p/CT x pieces)	61,200 sec = 1,020 min	60,600 sec = 1,010 min
Time available/day for changeovers	1,056 total minutes -1,020 min for run 36 min for all changeovers	1,122 total minutes - 1,010 min for run 112 min for all changeovers
Divided by changeovers required/day	36/0.5 = 72 min/changeover	112/8 = 14 min/changeover
Summary of Target Condition		
Cycle time per piece	120 seconds	100 seconds
Unplanned downtime	20 %	15 %
Changeover time	72 minutes	14 minutes

Steve

In mathematically developing the target condition for the small gear machining loop, Steve lands on **three themes**, which will become challenges for the individual processes inside that value stream loop: Achieving a cycle time of 100 seconds/piece, an unplanned downtime of 15 percent or less, and a changeover time of 14 minutes. When these numbers are achieved, the 3-day lead time is possible for small-gear machining.

As Steve explains his thinking, Nancy learns not only what Steve's target condition is, but also about the thinking process behind it. As a result, she is confident that Steve isn't just guessing at his numbers. Steve is effectively teaching Nancy how he worked through this, and she recognizes that he has a deep understanding. So this is about more than just the numbers: the coach and learner are developing a shared understanding and consensus about what must be achieved and why.

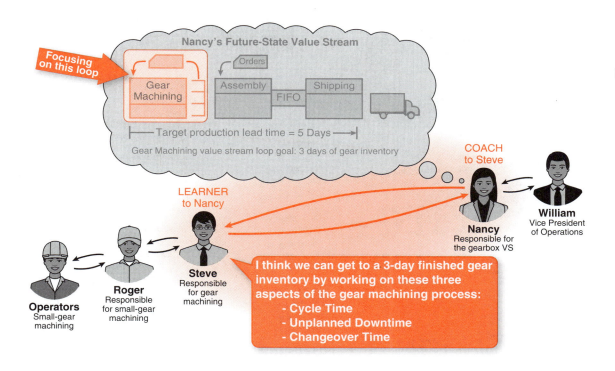

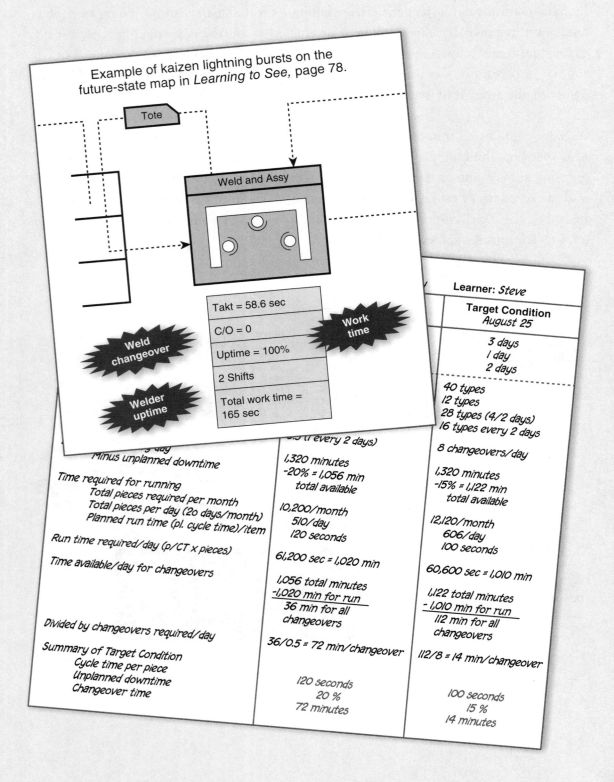

Example of kaizen lightning bursts on the future-state map in *Learning to See*, page 78.

Tote

Weld and Assy

Takt = 58.6 sec	
C/O = 0	
Uptime = 100%	
2 Shifts	
Total work time = 165 sec	

Weld changeover

Work time

Welder uptime

Learner: *Steve*

Target Condition
August 25

3 days
1 day
2 days

40 types
12 types
28 types (4/2 days)
16 types every 2 days

8 changeovers/day

1,320 minutes
-15% = 1,122 min
total available

12,120/month
606/day
100 seconds

60,600 sec = 1,010 min

1,122 total minutes
- 1,010 min for run
112 min for all
changeovers

112/8 = 14 min/changeover

100 seconds
15 %
14 minutes

...g day
Minus unplanned downtime

Time required for running
   Total pieces required per month
   Total pieces per day (20 days/month)
   Planned run time (pl. cycle time)/item

Run time required/day (p/CT x pieces)

Time available/day for changeovers

Divided by changeovers required/day

Summary of Target Condition
   Cycle time per piece
   Unplanned downtime
   Changeover time

0.5 (1 every 2 days)

1,320 minutes
-20% = 1,056 min
total available

10,200/month
510/day
120 seconds

61,200 sec = 1,020 min

1,056 total minutes
-1,020 min for run
36 min for all
changeovers

36/0.5 = 72 min/changeover

120 seconds
20 %
72 minutes

Nancy now adds these process-level themes, or necessary process improvements, as "kaizen lightning bursts" on her future-state value stream map. This is the correct use of the kaizen burst icon in Value Stream Mapping.

Since the value stream map is a central communication tool and all team members and learners working for Nancy should know what their contribution is, the kaizen lightning bursts give an overview of the focused improvement activities along the value stream that are aimed at achieving the future-state design.

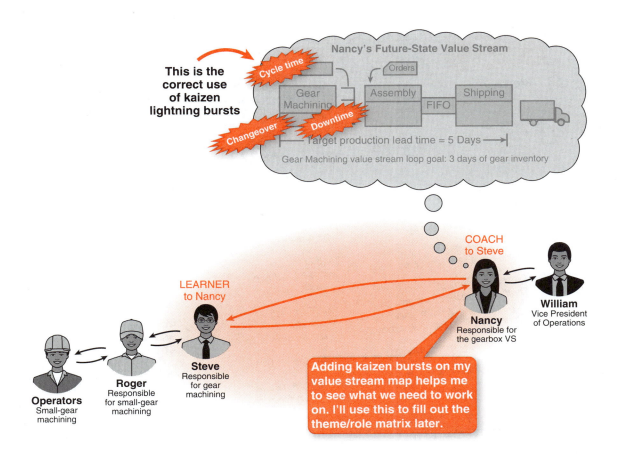

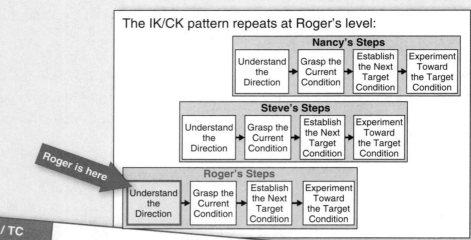

The IK/CK pattern repeats at Roger's level:

Nancy's Steps

| Understand the Direction | → | Grasp the Current Condition | → | Establish the Next Target Condition | → | Experiment Toward the Target Condition |

Steve's Steps

| Understand the Direction | → | Grasp the Current Condition | → | Establish the Next Target Condition | → | Experiment Toward the Target Condition |

Roger is here →

Roger's Steps

| Understand the Direction | → | Grasp the Current Condition | → | Establish the Next Target Condition | → | Experiment Toward the Target Condition |

CC / TC Form

Process: *Small-Gear Machining*   Coach: *Nancy*   Learner: *Steve*

Category	Current Condition May 17	Target Condition August 25
Stock	30 days	3 days
Safety factor	10 days	1 day
EPEI (time to cycle through all parts)	20 days	2 days
Total types	30 types	40 types
Runners	8 types	12 types
Specials	22 types (2/20 days)	28 types (4/2 days)
Total types every EPEI	10 types every 20 days	16 types every 2 days
Changeovers required every day	0.5 (1 every 2 days)	8 changeovers/day
Time available every day	1,320 minutes	1,320 minutes
Minus unplanned downtime	-20% = 1,056 min total available	-15% = 1,122 min total available
Time required for running		
Total pieces required per month	10,200/month	12,120/month
Total pieces per day (20 days/month)	510/day	606/day
Planned run time (pl. cycle time)/item	120 seconds	100 seconds
Run time required/day (p/CT x pieces)	61,200 sec = 1,020 min	60,600 sec = 1,010 min
Time available/day for changeovers	1,056 total minutes −1,020 min for run 36 min for all changeovers	1,122 total minutes − 1,010 min for run 112 min for all changeovers
Divided by changeovers required/day	36/0.5 = 72 min/changeover	112/8 = 14 min/changeover
Summary of Target Condition		
Cycle time per piece	120 seconds	100 seconds
Unplanned downtime	20 %	15 %
Changeover time	72 minutes	14 minutes

Steve

Next Level Down:
Roger Works at the *Process* Level

Steve decides to have his learner **Roger** first work on the changeover time challenge at one of the selected small-gear machines. At this point the Improvement Kata steps repeat, one level down. Steve's other learners, Rachel and Robert, will address the downtime and cycle time themes on other small-gear machining processes.

Although Roger is given a significant challenge by Steve, his coach and boss, Roger can see from the future-state value stream map and CC/TC form why his support is needed. Since his coach offers support at all times, he feels valued, respected, and motivated to help.

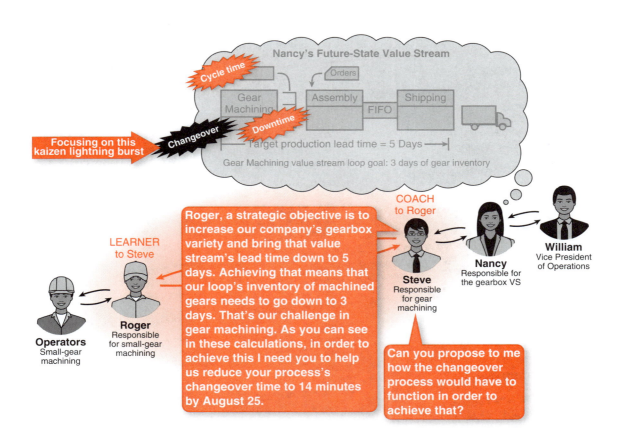

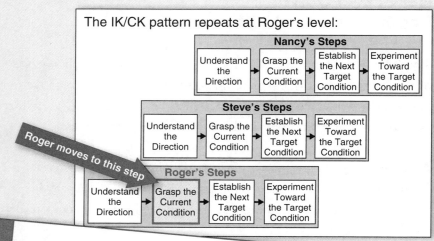

The IK/CK pattern repeats at Roger's level:

Nancy's Steps

Understand the Direction → Grasp the Current Condition → Establish the Next Target Condition → Experiment Toward the Target Condition

Steve's Steps

Understand the Direction → Grasp the Current Condition → Establish the Next Target Condition → Experiment Toward the Target Condition

Roger moves to this step

Roger's Steps

Understand the Direction → Grasp the Current Condition → Establish the Next Target Condition → Experiment Toward the Target Condition

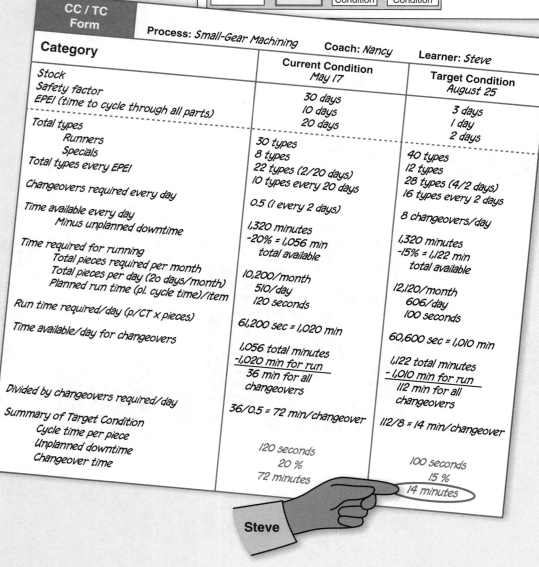

CC / TC Form

Process: *Small-Gear Machining*　　Coach: *Nancy*　　Learner: *Steve*

Category	Current Condition May 17	Target Condition August 25
Stock		
Safety factor		
EPEI (time to cycle through all parts)	30 days	
	10 days	3 days
	20 days	1 day
Total types		2 days
Runners	30 types	
Specials	8 types	40 types
Total types every EPEI	22 types (2/20 days)	12 types
	10 types every 20 days	28 types (4/2 days)
Changeovers required every day		16 types every 2 days
	0.5 (1 every 2 days)	
Time available every day		8 changeovers/day
Minus unplanned downtime	1,320 minutes	
	-20% = 1,056 min	1,320 minutes
Time required for running	total available	-15% = 1,122 min
Total pieces required per month		total available
Total pieces per day (20 days/month)	10,200/month	
Planned run time (pl. cycle time)/item	510/day	12,120/month
	120 seconds	606/day
Run time required/day (p/CT x pieces)		100 seconds
Time available/day for changeovers	61,200 sec = 1,020 min	
		60,600 sec = 1,010 min
	1,056 total minutes	
	-1,020 min for run	1,122 total minutes
	36 min for all	- 1,010 min for run
	changeovers	112 min for all
Divided by changeovers required/day		changeovers
	36/0.5 = 72 min/changeover	112/8 = 14 min/changeover
Summary of Target Condition		
Cycle time per piece	120 seconds	100 seconds
Unplanned downtime	20 %	15 %
Changeover time	72 minutes	14 minutes

Steve

In his coaching, Steve is not telling Roger how to achieve the challenge. No one knows that exactly. Steve's coaching focuses instead on Roger's practice of the systematic, scientific pattern of the Improvement Kata.

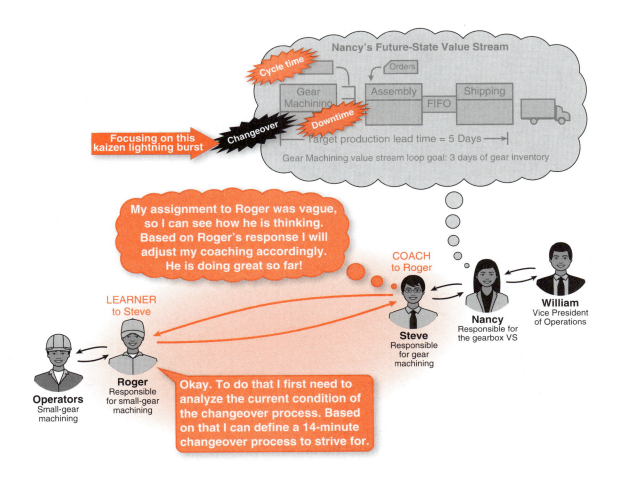

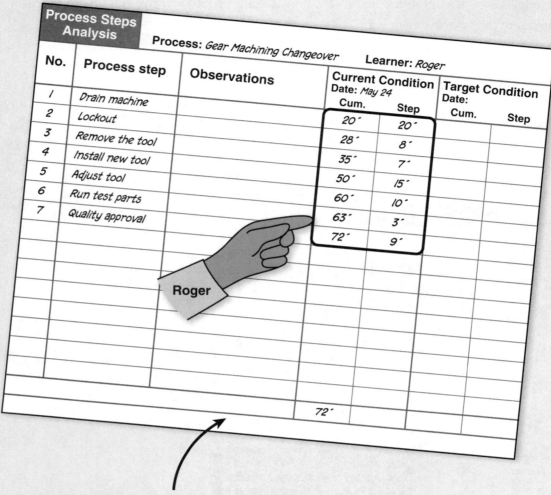

Process Steps Analysis	Process: *Gear Machining Changeover*		Learner: *Roger*			
No.	Process step	Observations	Current Condition Date: *May 24*		Target Condition Date:	
			Cum.	Step	Cum.	Step
1	Drain machine		20´	20´		
2	Lockout		28´	8´		
3	Remove the tool		35´	7´		
4	Install new tool		50´	15´		
5	Adjust tool		60´	10´		
6	Run test parts		63´	3´		
7	Quality approval		72´	9´		
		Roger				
			72´			

Note: Roger is using this form as his current condition/target condition form

Two Days Later . . .

Roger has conducted a process analysis by observing several changeovers at his process, recording the steps and times of the changeover process, and preparing a run chart of the total changeover times. Roger is grasping the **initial current condition** of the changeover process.

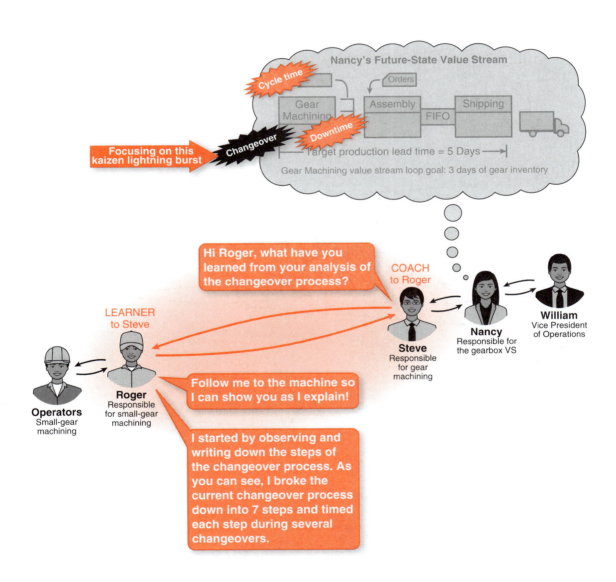

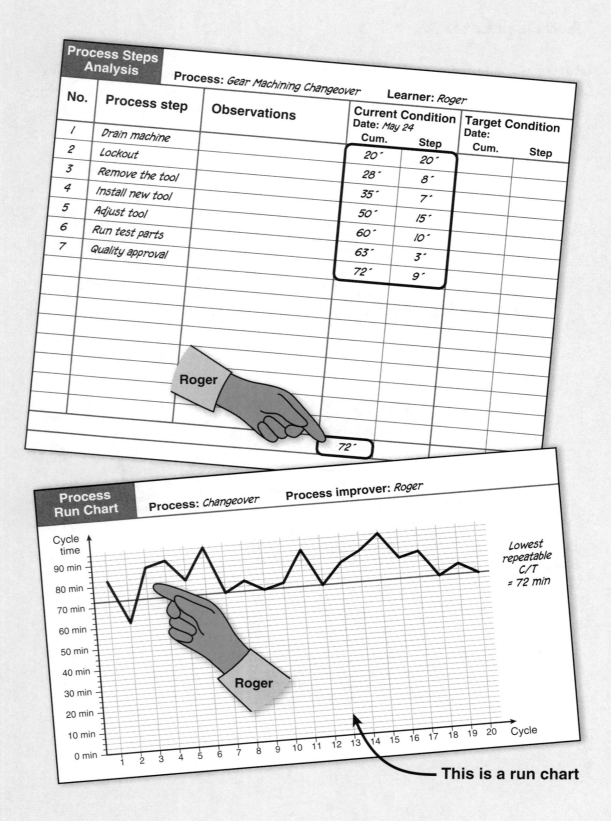

Process Steps Analysis

Process: *Gear Machining Changeover* Learner: *Roger*

No.	Process step	Observations	Current Condition Date: *May 24*		Target Condition Date:	
			Cum.	Step	Cum.	Step
1	Drain machine		20´	20´		
2	Lockout		28´	8´		
3	Remove the tool		35´	7´		
4	Install new tool		50´	15´		
5	Adjust tool		60´	10´		
6	Run test parts		63´	3´		
7	Quality approval		72´	9´		

Roger

72´

Process Run Chart

Process: *Changeover* Process improver: *Roger*

Cycle time

90 min
80 min
70 min
60 min
50 min
40 min
30 min
20 min
10 min
0 min

1 2 3 4 5 6 7 8 9 10 11 12 13 14 15 16 17 18 19 20 Cycle

Lowest repeatable C/T = 72 min

Roger

This is a run chart

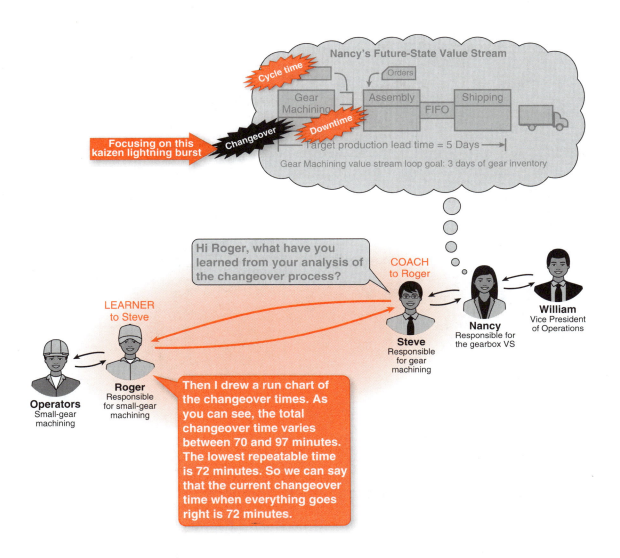

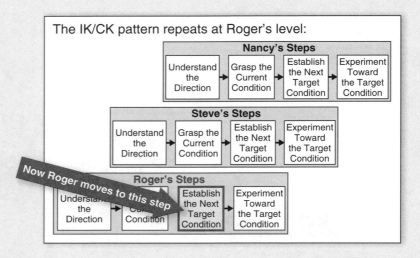

The IK/CK pattern repeats at Roger's level:

Nancy's Steps
Understand the Direction → Grasp the Current Condition → Establish the Next Target Condition → Experiment Toward the Target Condition

Steve's Steps
Understand the Direction → Grasp the Current Condition → Establish the Next Target Condition → Experiment Toward the Target Condition

Now Roger moves to this step

Roger's Steps
Understand the Direction → Current Condition → Establish the Next Target Condition → Experiment Toward the Target Condition

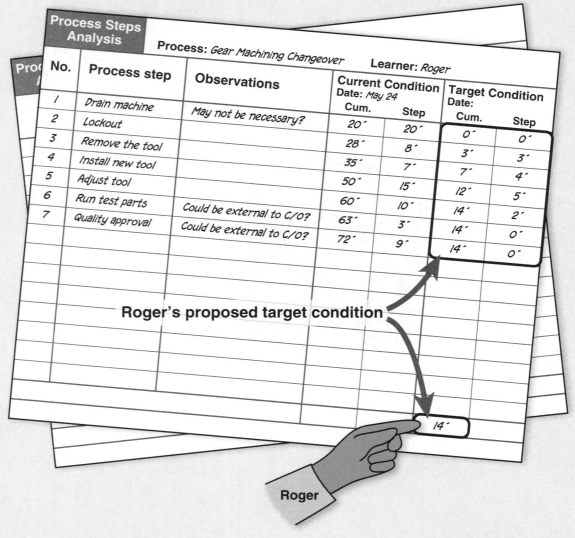

Process Steps Analysis

Process: *Gear Machining Changeover*   Learner: *Roger*

No.	Process step	Observations	Current Condition Date: *May 24*		Target Condition Date:	
			Cum.	Step	Cum.	Step
1	Drain machine	May not be necessary?	20˝	20˝	0˝	0˝
2	Lockout		28˝	8˝	3˝	3˝
3	Remove the tool		35˝	7˝	7˝	4˝
4	Install new tool		50˝	15˝	12˝	5˝
5	Adjust tool		60˝	10˝	14˝	2˝
6	Run test parts	Could be external to C/O?	63˝	3˝	14˝	0˝
7	Quality approval	Could be external to C/O?	72˝	9˝	14˝	0˝

Roger's proposed target condition

14˝

Roger

Roger Proposes a Target Condition

Based on his process analysis, Roger proposes a target condition for the changeover process at his gear machining process. However, Steve provides a corrective feedback.

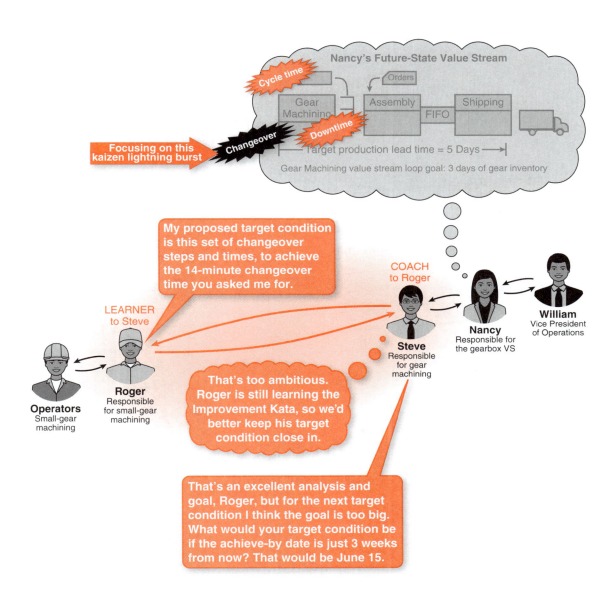

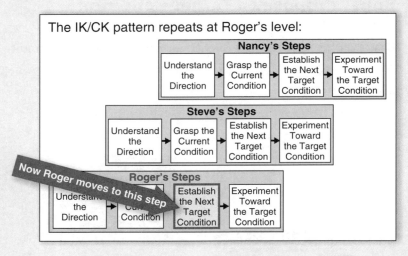

The IK/CK pattern repeats at Roger's level:

Nancy's Steps

Understand the Direction → Grasp the Current Condition → Establish the Next Target Condition → Experiment Toward the Target Condition

Steve's Steps

Understand the Direction → Grasp the Current Condition → Establish the Next Target Condition → Experiment Toward the Target Condition

Now Roger moves to this step

Roger's Steps

Understand the Direction → Current Condition → Establish the Next Target Condition → Experiment Toward the Target Condition

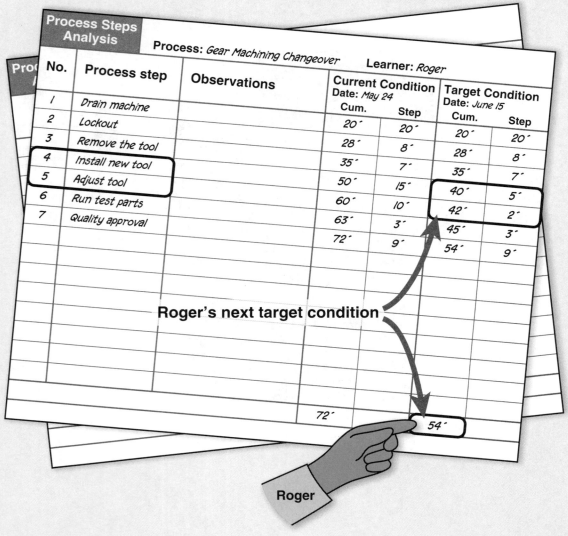

Process Steps Analysis

Process: *Gear Machining Changeover*   Learner: *Roger*

No.	Process step	Observations	Current Condition Date: May 24 Cum.	Step	Target Condition Date: June 15 Cum.	Step
1	Drain machine					
2	Lockout		20˝	20˝	20˝	20˝
3	Remove the tool		28˝	8˝	28˝	8˝
4	Install new tool		35˝	7˝	35˝	7˝
5	Adjust tool		50˝	15˝	40˝	5˝
6	Run test parts		60˝	10˝	42˝	2˝
7	Quality approval		63˝	3˝	45˝	3˝
			72˝	9˝	54˝	9˝
		72˝			54˝	

Roger's next target condition

Roger

Agreeing on Roger's Next Target Condition

Considering the three week achieve-by date, Roger proposes a more modest next target condition. Steve agrees, and thus this learner's next target condition is established.

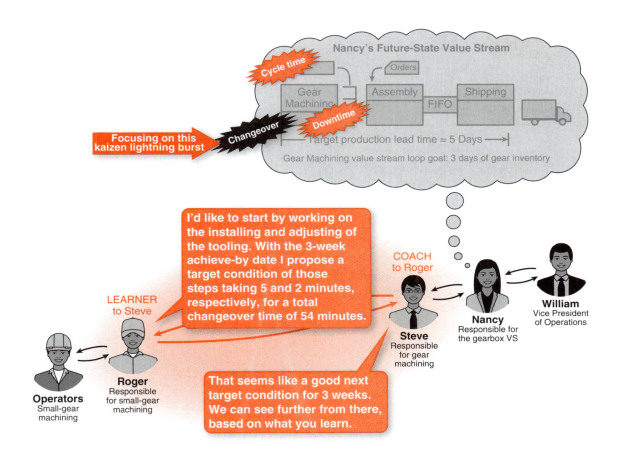

Within the gear machining loop Steve has three learners, each working on a different aspect of the gear machining loop target condition. For the sake of clarity, in the coaching cycle dialogues that follow we will show only Steve's coaching of Roger.

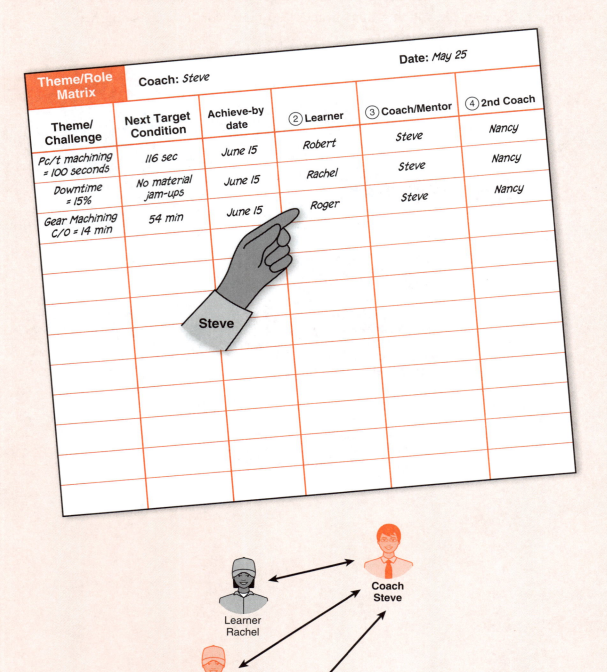

Theme/Role Matrix	Coach: *Steve*				Date: *May 25*
Theme/ Challenge	Next Target Condition	Achieve-by date	② Learner	③ Coach/Mentor	④ 2nd Coach
Pc/t machining = 100 seconds	116 sec	June 15	Robert	Steve	Nancy
Downtime = 15%	No material jam-ups	June 15	Rachel	Steve	Nancy
Gear Machining C/O = 14 min	54 min	June 15	Roger	Steve	Nancy

Steve

Learner Rachel

Coach Steve

Learner Roger

Learner Robert

Steve Defines Roles by Theme for His *Value Stream Loop*

As Steve and his learners agree on their target conditions, those target conditions are summarized in a table, which helps the coach keep an overview and allocate their coaching time.

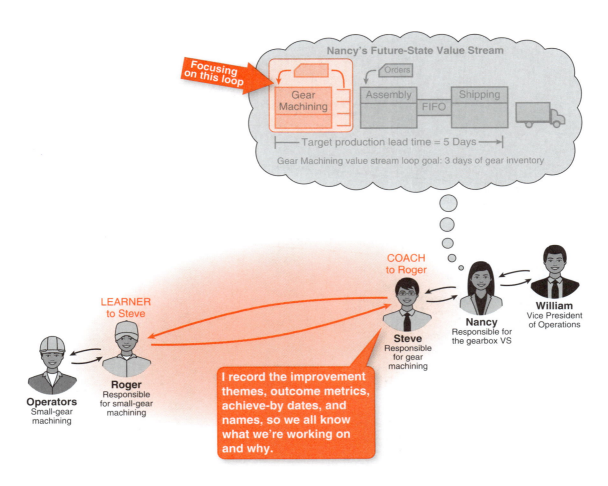

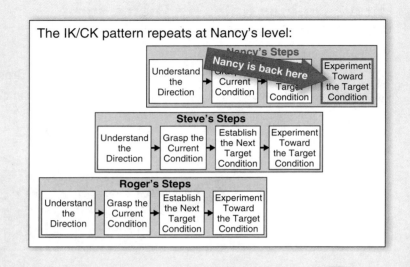

The IK/CK pattern repeats at Nancy's level:

Nancy's Steps

Understand the Direction → Grasp the Current Condition → Target Condition → Experiment Toward the Target Condition

Nancy is back here

Steve's Steps

Understand the Direction → Grasp the Current Condition → Establish the Next Target Condition → Experiment Toward the Target Condition

Roger's Steps

Understand the Direction → Grasp the Current Condition → Establish the Next Target Condition → Experiment Toward the Target Condition

Date: *May 25*

Theme/Role Matrix	Coach: *Nancy*				
Theme/ Challenge	**Next Target Condition**	**Achieve-by date**	② **Learner**	③ **Coach/Mentor**	④ **2nd Coach**
Pc/t machining = 100 seconds	*116 sec*	*June 15*	*Robert*	*Steve*	*Nancy*
Downtime = 15%	*No material jam-ups*	*June 15*	*Rachel*	*Steve*	*Nancy*
Gear Machining C/O = 14 min	*54 min*	*June 15*	*Roger*	*Steve*	*Nancy*
T.B.D.	*T.B.D.*	*T.B.D.*	*T.B.D.*	*Scott*	*Nancy*
T.B.D.	*T.B.D.*	*T.B.D.*	*T.B.D.*	*Scott*	*Nancy*
T.B.D.	*T.B.D.*	*T.B.D.*	*T.B.D.*	*Scott*	*Nancy*
T.B.D.	*T.B.D.*	*T.B.D.*	*T.B.D.*	*Sarah*	*Nancy*
T.B.D.	*T.B.D.*	*T.B.D.*	*T.B.D.*	*Sarah*	*Nancy*
T.B.D.	*T.B.D.*	*T.B.D.*	*T.B.D.*	*Sarah*	*Nancy*
T.B.D.	*T.B.D.*	*T.B.D.*	*T.B.D.*	*Sean*	*Nancy*
T.B.D.	*T.B.D.*	*T.B.D.*	*T.B.D.*	*Sean*	*Nancy*
T.B.D.	*T.B.D.*	*T.B.D.*	*T.B.D.*		

Nancy Summarizes These Roles at the *Value Stream* Level

At the value stream level, the themes from each value stream loop are summarized by Nancy. With this she has an overview of the improvement activities being coached by the managers in her value stream that are aimed at the future-state value stream design.

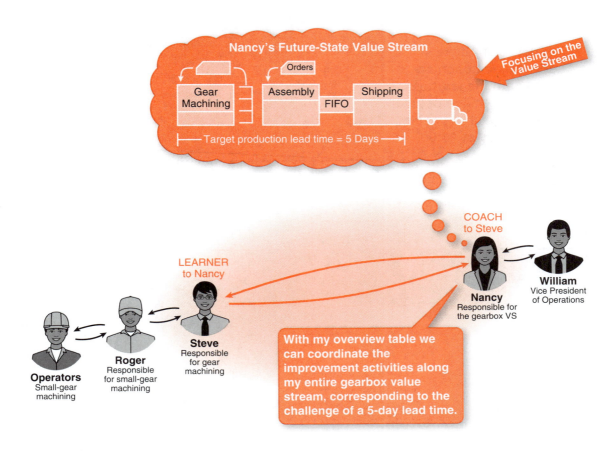

57

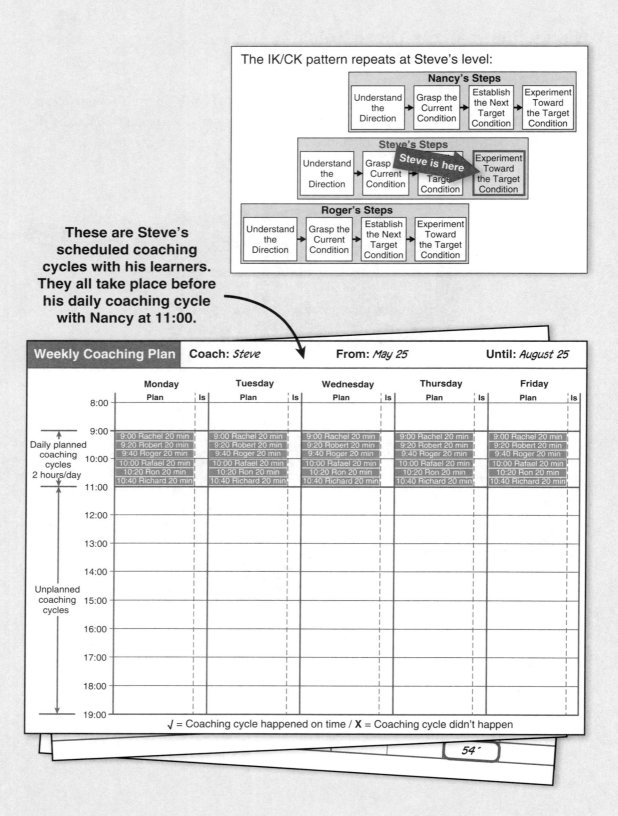

The IK/CK pattern repeats at Steve's level:

Nancy's Steps

Understand the Direction → Grasp the Current Condition → Establish the Next Target Condition → Experiment Toward the Target Condition

Steve's Steps

Understand the Direction → Grasp Current Condition → Target Condition — *Steve is here* → Experiment Toward the Target Condition

Roger's Steps

Understand the Direction → Grasp the Current Condition → Establish the Next Target Condition → Experiment Toward the Target Condition

These are Steve's scheduled coaching cycles with his learners. They all take place before his daily coaching cycle with Nancy at 11:00.

Weekly Coaching Plan **Coach:** *Steve*   **From:** *May 25*   **Until:** *August 25*

	Monday Plan	Is	Tuesday Plan	Is	Wednesday Plan	Is	Thursday Plan	Is	Friday Plan	Is
8:00										
9:00	9:00 Rachel 20 min		9:00 Rachel 20 min		9:00 Rachel 20 min		9:00 Rachel 20 min		9:00 Rachel 20 min	
	9:20 Robert 20 min		9:20 Robert 20 min		9:20 Robert 20 min		9:20 Robert 20 min		9:20 Robert 20 min	
	9:40 Roger 20 min		9:40 Roger 20 min		9:40 Roger 20 min		9:40 Roger 20 min		9:40 Roger 20 min	
10:00	10:00 Rafael 20 min		10:00 Rafael 20 min		10:00 Rafael 20 min		10:00 Rafael 20 min		10:00 Rafael 20 min	
	10:20 Ron 20 min		10:20 Ron 20 min		10:20 Ron 20 min		10:20 Ron 20 min		10:20 Ron 20 min	
	10:40 Richard 20 min		10:40 Richard 20 min		10:40 Richard 20 min		10:40 Richard 20 min		10:40 Richard 20 min	
11:00										
12:00										
13:00										
14:00										
15:00										
16:00										
17:00										
18:00										
19:00										

Daily planned coaching cycles 2 hours/day

Unplanned coaching cycles

√ = Coaching cycle happened on time / X = Coaching cycle didn't happen

54´

Steve

Establish the Schedule for Coaching Cycles

Steve has a daily schedule of defined coaching cycle appointments between 9:00 and 11:00 a.m. The scheduled coaching cycles are the trigger for Steve to practice his coaching skills. Additional coaching cycles can be done as needed.

Coaching cycles are scheduled "bottom up" to ensure fast upward communication of learnings. This means that process-level coaching cycles are done first each day, and William's coaching cycle with Nancy is done last. So, within just hours, all learnings become available at the senior management level. This allows for fast reaction and adaptation if needed, since quick, subtle corrections are necessary to keep everyone's efforts aligned when so many steps are being done in parallel.

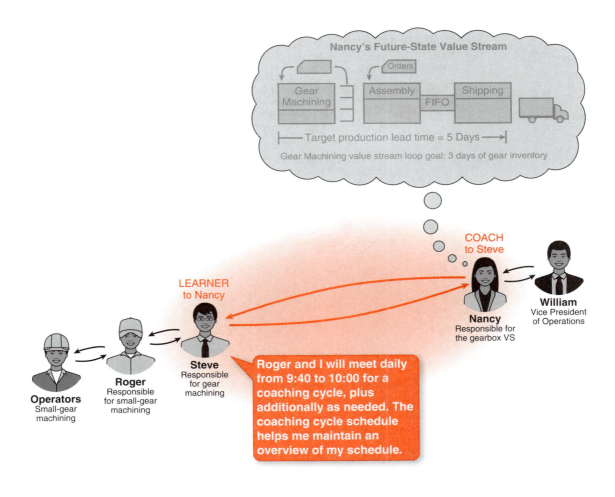

Summary So Far—Planning Phase

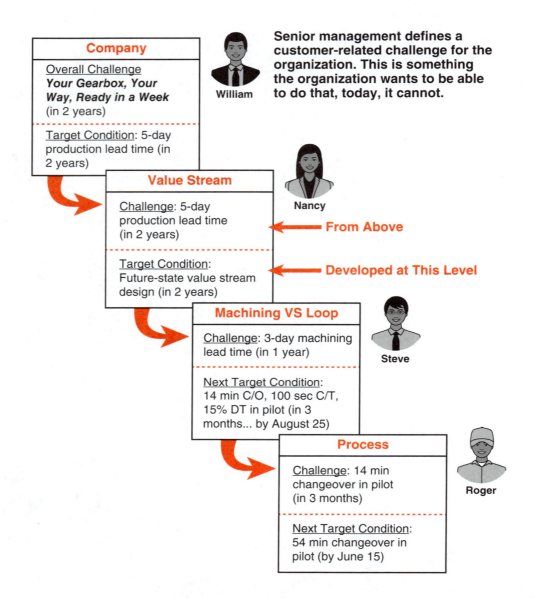

Company

Overall Challenge
Your Gearbox, Your Way, Ready in a Week
(in 2 years)

Target Condition: 5-day production lead time (in 2 years)

William

Senior management defines a customer-related challenge for the organization. This is something the organization wants to be able to do that, today, it cannot.

Nancy

Value Stream

Challenge: 5-day production lead time (in 2 years)

← **From Above**

Target Condition: Future-state value stream design (in 2 years)

← **Developed at This Level**

Machining VS Loop

Challenge: 3-day machining lead time (in 1 year)

Next Target Condition: 14 min C/O, 100 sec C/T, 15% DT in pilot (in 3 months... by August 25)

Steve

Roger

Process

Challenge: 14 min changeover in pilot (in 3 months)

Next Target Condition: 54 min changeover in pilot (by June 15)

So far we've shown you the three planning steps of the Improvement Kata pattern. This part of the Improvement Kata may not be as exciting as the executing phase, but it is vitally important for working in a scientific, goal-directed manner. Never skip it!

In your practice you will find that the steps of the Improvement Kata are not entirely separate and linear. For instance, things that you learn in the executing phase will feed back into your plan, as indicated by the sawtooth line below. This is normal.

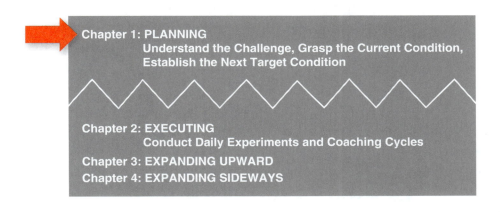

Chapter 1: PLANNING
    Understand the Challenge, Grasp the Current Condition,
    Establish the Next Target Condition

Chapter 2: EXECUTING
    Conduct Daily Experiments and Coaching Cycles

Chapter 3: EXPANDING UPWARD
Chapter 4: EXPANDING SIDEWAYS

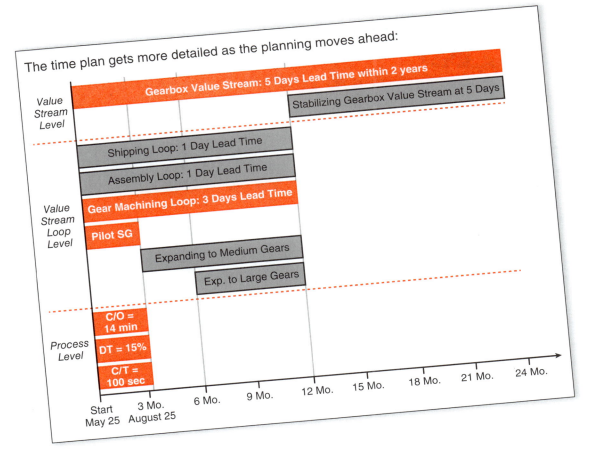

The time plan gets more detailed as the planning moves ahead:

Now it's time to execute, focused and fast.

CHAPTER 2

EXECUTING

Conduct Daily Experiments and Coaching Cycles

About the Executing Phase Chapter

Working like a Scientist to Reach the Next Target Condition

Having a next target condition (in consideration of the current condition and aimed at the challenge) as developed in the previous chapter is important, but great execution is equally important. If you bring those two together then just about anything is possible.

In this chapter, the learner now strives toward their next target condition iteratively through experiments, while the coach accompanies that process and gives input on Improvement Kata procedure, via 20-minute daily coaching cycles based on the five Coaching Kata questions.

Keep in mind that coaching cycles are not a method to implement, but a teaching process for continually assessing and building Improvement Kata capability in the organization. The format for conducting coaching cycles is a Starter Kata.

Understand the
Direction or Challenge

Grasp the
Current Condition

Establish the
Next Target Condition

EXECUTING
Experiment Toward
the Target Condition

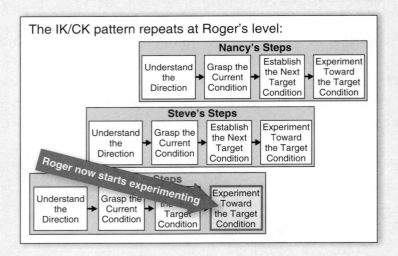

The IK/CK pattern repeats at Roger's level:

A typical coaching cycle at a learner's storyboard

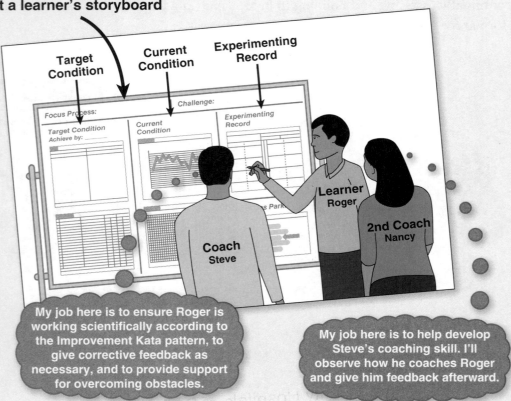

My job here is to ensure Roger is working scientifically according to the Improvement Kata pattern, to give corrective feedback as necessary, and to provide support for overcoming obstacles.

My job here is to help develop Steve's coaching skill. I'll observe how he coaches Roger and give him feedback afterward.

Steve Coaches Roger Daily Toward His Changeover Time Target Condition

Steve and Roger meet for at least one scheduled coaching cycle every day. A coaching cycle usually takes 20 minutes or less.

During the coaching cycles at his storyboard, Roger begins by reviewing the challenge, target condition, and the current condition that exists now. Using his *experimenting record (a Starter Kata)*, Roger then describes his learnings from the last experiment against the current obstacle, his proposed next step (next experiment), and the predicted result from taking that step—all by responding to the coach's series of Coaching Kata questions.

Note that Roger prepares these details in writing on his storyboard *before* the coaching cycle. This is important because it helps Steve to see how Roger is currently thinking about the improvement process and thus where Roger might need coaching input. The coach is trying to spot if and where the learner is not working scientifically, so that the coach can provide appropriate situational feedback. The five Coaching Kata questions are scripted, but the feedback is not.

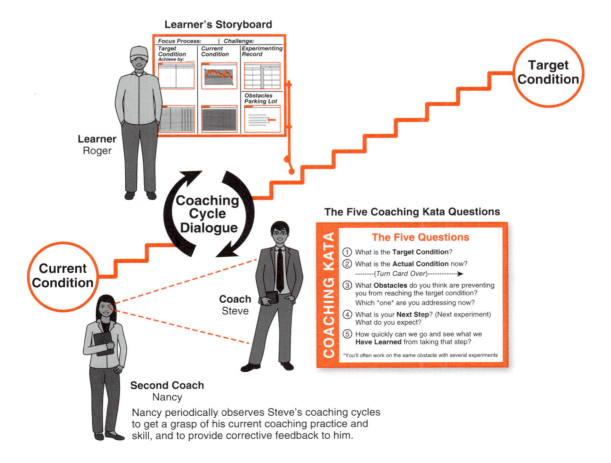

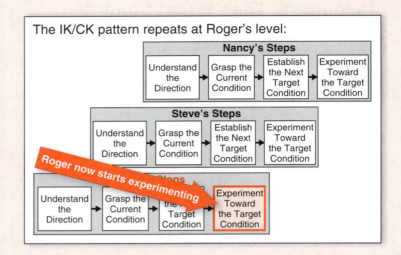

The IK/CK pattern repeats at Roger's level:

The schedule for Steve's coaching cycles

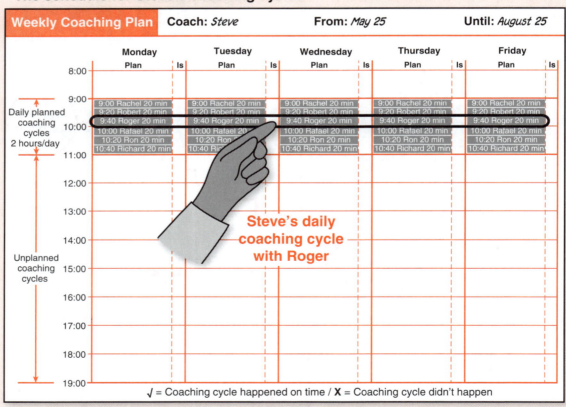

Steve's daily coaching cycle with Roger

Having frequent (daily) coaching cycles leads Roger to take small steps between coaching cycles, thereby learning faster and adjusting faster based on what he is learning. This lowers the risk of Roger working based on false assumptions or practicing incorrect Improvement Kata procedure for too long. Having daily coaching cycles also helps Roger realize that his work is meaningful.

When a coaching chain is established and running—with regular coaching cycles going on at every level—learnings and the resulting small adjustments can be communicated quickly, which keeps information flowing up and down the hierarchy.

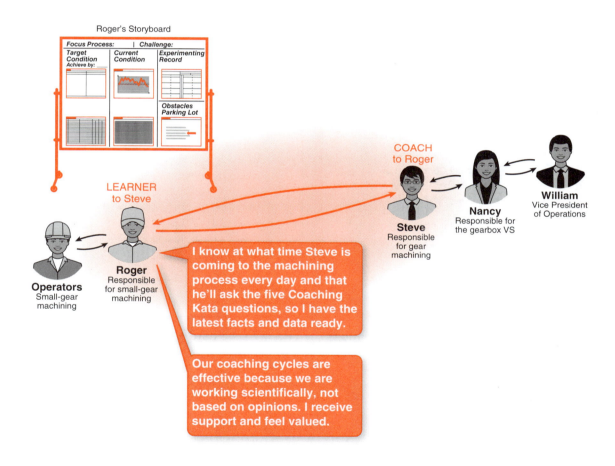

The Coach's Main Starter Kata:
The Five Question Card

Each coaching cycle is built around the framework of the five Coaching Kata questions, which are utilized in the coaching cycles up and down the organization. The five Coaching Kata questions are the main headings of a coaching cycle. Of course, the coach can also ask clarifying questions in between the five questions. More on that in the Conclusion. In the coaching cycle dialogues that follow, for simplicity's sake we'll concentrate mainly on the five Coaching Kata questions.

Here is the coach's Starter Kata five question card:

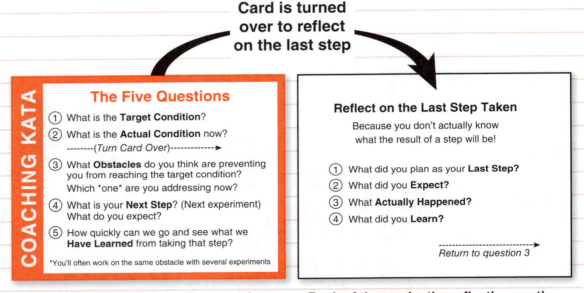

Card is turned over to reflect on the last step

COACHING KATA

The Five Questions

① What is the **Target Condition**?
② What is the **Actual Condition** now?
--------(Turn Card Over)------------→
③ What **Obstacles** do you think are preventing you from reaching the target condition? Which *one* are you addressing now?
④ What is your **Next Step**? (Next experiment) What do you expect?
⑤ How quickly can we go and see what we **Have Learned** from taking that step?

*You'll often work on the same obstacle with several experiments

Reflect on the Last Step Taken
Because you don't actually know what the result of a step will be!

① What did you plan as your **Last Step?**
② What did you **Expect?**
③ What **Actually Happened?**
④ What did you **Learn?**

-------------------------→
Return to question 3

Front of the card with the five questions   **Back of the card = the reflection section**

Source: The Toyota Kata Practice Guide

The five Coaching Kata questions have two main purposes:

1. To reinforce the scientific pattern of the Improvement Kata. The learner knows what basic questions the coach will ask in the next coaching cycle and prepares their information on the storyboard accordingly.

2. To help the coach see how the learner is thinking. The coach's job is to provide corrective procedural inputs, to ensure that the learner is proceeding (practicing) according to the scientific pattern of the Improvement Kata. However, the coach cannot provide such feedback until the learner has said or done something, which then shows how the learner is currently thinking. The five questions are prompts for the learner to respond to and thereby help make the learner's thinking visible. This is also why the learner updates and prepares the storyboard *before* the coaching cycle.

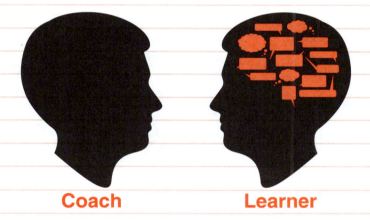

Coach   **Learner**

Source: The Toyota Kata Practice Guide

COACHING KATA

The Five Questions

1. What is the **Target Condition**?

2. What is the **Actual Condition** now?

   --------(Turn Card Over)-------------->

3. What **Obstacles** do you think are preventing you from reaching the target condition?
   Which *one* are you addressing now?

4. What is your **Next Step**? (Next experiment)
   What do you expect?

5. How quickly can we go and see what we **Have Learned** from taking that step?

*You'll often work on the same obstacle with several experiments

Steve

Process Steps Analysis

Process: Gear Machining Changeover   **Learner:** Roger

No.	Process step	Observations	Current Condition Date: May 24 Cum.	Step	Target Condition Date: June 15 Cum.	Step
			20´	20´	20´	20´
1	Drain machine		28´	8´	28´	8´
2	Lockout		35´	7´	35´	7´
3	Remove the tool		50´	15´	40´	5´
4	Install new tool		60´	10´	42´	2´
5	Adjust tool		63´	3´	45´	3´
6	Run test parts		72´	9´	54´	9´
7	Quality approval					
			72´		54´	

Roger

Roger's target condition

Steve and Roger Meet Daily at Roger's Storyboard

The coaching cycles start and end at the learner's storyboard, which is usually near the focus process. The coach holds the **five question card** in their hand. The coach begins by asking the learner to state the challenge and then gets into the five Coaching Kata questions.

The learner points to relevant information and supporting documents that have been posted—in advance of the coaching cycle—on their storyboard. A pencil and eraser are kept at hand because adjustments might be made to the storyboard materials during the coaching cycle dialogue. If possible, the coach and learner should also go and see the situation at the focus process firsthand. Stay grounded in facts as much as you can.

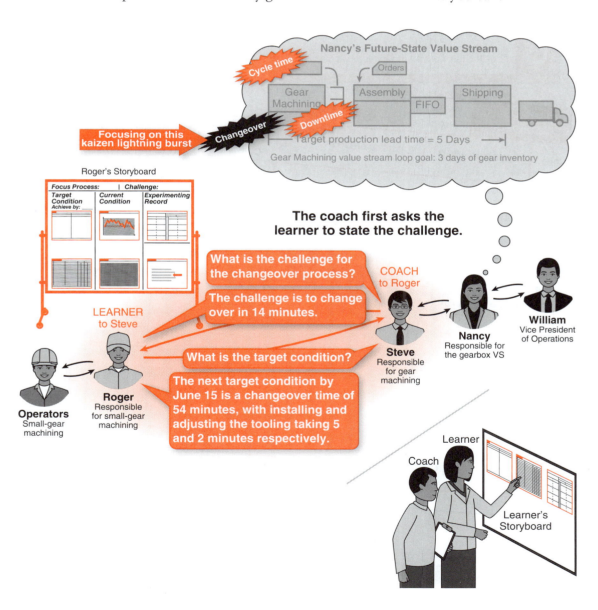

COACHING KATA

The Five Questions

1. What is the **Target Condition**?
2. What is the **Actual Condition** now?
   --------(Turn Card Over)------------→
3. What **Obstacles** do you think are preventing you from reaching the target condition?
   Which *one* are you addressing now?
4. What is your **Next Step**? (Next experiment) What do you expect?
5. How quickly can we go and see what we **Have Learned** from taking that step?

*You'll often work on the same obstacle with several experiments

Steve

Process Steps Analysis			Current Condition Date: May 24		Target Condition Date: June 15	
	Process: Gear Machining Changeover				Learner: Roger	
No.	Process step	Observations	Cum.	Step	Cum.	Step
			20´	20´	20´	20´
1	Drain machine		28´	8´	28´	8´
2	Lockout		35´	7´	35´	7´
3	Remove the tool		50´	15´	40´	5´
4	Install new tool		60´	10´	42´	2´
5	Adjust tool		63´	3´	45´	3´
6	Run test parts		72´	9´	54´	9´
7	Quality approval					
			72´		54´	

Roger

Roger

Remember that to grasp the initial current condition of the changeover process, Roger conducted a detailed process analysis. Here he points to the changeover steps, sequence, times, and run chart on his storyboard.

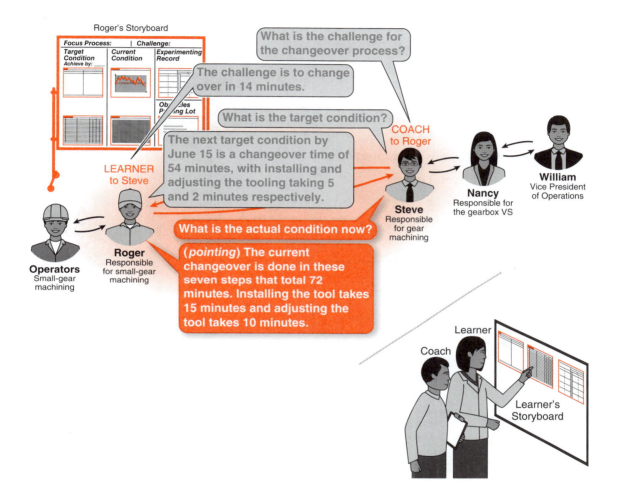

The coach now uses the reflection section on the back of the card.

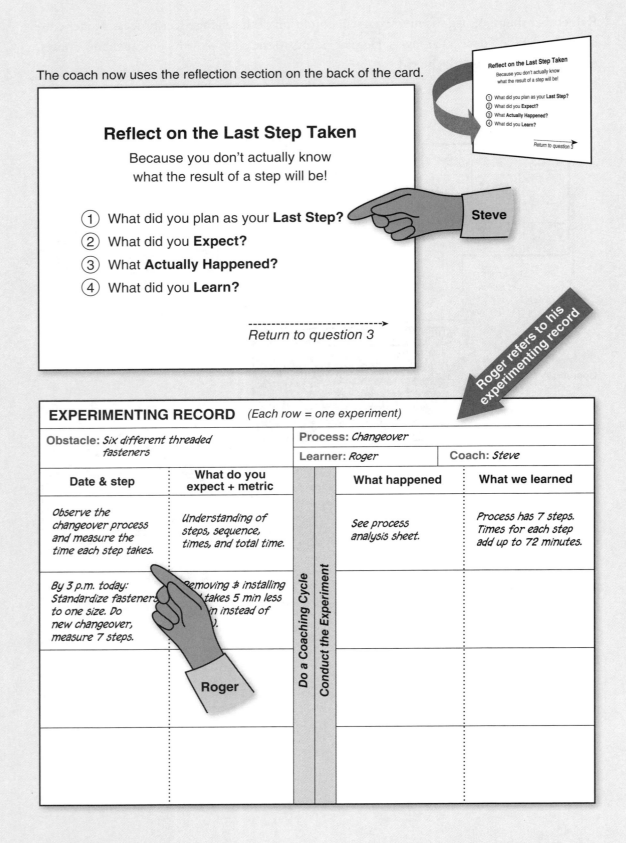

Reflect on the Last Step Taken

Because you don't actually know
what the result of a step will be!

① What did you plan as your **Last Step?** ← Steve

② What did you **Expect?**

③ What **Actually Happened?**

④ What did you **Learn?**

- - - - - - - - - - - - - - - - - - →
Return to question 3

Reflect on the Last Step Taken
Because you don't actually know
what the result of a step will be!

① What did you plan as your **Last Step?**
② What did you **Expect?**
③ What **Actually Happened?**
④ What did you **Learn?**

Return to question 3 →

Roger refers to his experimenting record

EXPERIMENTING RECORD (*Each row = one experiment*)

Obstacle: *Six different threaded fasteners*			Process: *Changeover*	
			Learner: *Roger*	Coach: *Steve*
Date & step	**What do you expect + metric**		**What happened**	**What we learned**
Observe the changeover process and measure the time each step takes.	*Understanding of steps, sequence, times, and total time.*	Do a Coaching Cycle — Conduct the Experiment	*See process analysis sheet.*	*Process has 7 steps. Times for each step add up to 72 minutes.*
By 3 p.m. today: Standardize fasteners to one size. Do new changeover, measure 7 steps.	*Removing & installing takes 5 min less in instead of .* ← Roger			

74

Now the coach flips the five question card over, to use the reflection section on the back. The coach and learner reflect on the learner's last experiment by referring to the learner's **experimenting record**. This Starter Kata form is used to plan experiments, record what happens, and reflect on the experiment.

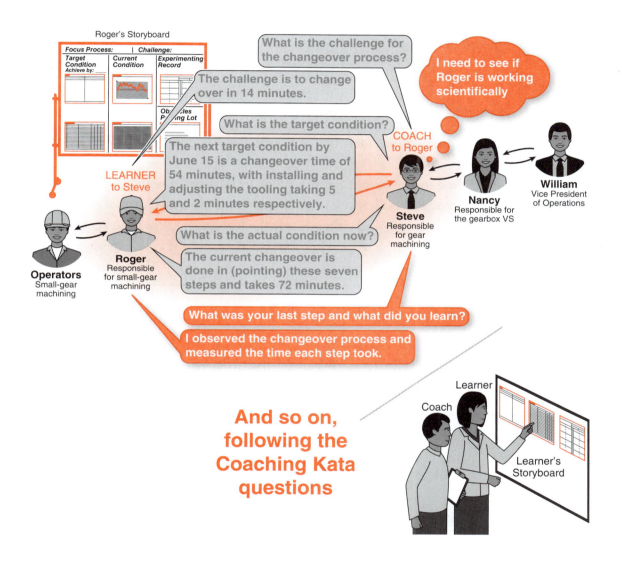

The Learner's Main Starter Kata in the Executing Phase: The Experimenting Record

The experimenting record is the learner's main practice routine for communicating their (a) reflections on the last experiment and (b) plan for the next experiment.

- Each experimenting record form is usually dedicated to one obstacle, and the learner will usually work on the same obstacle with several experiments. Separate forms are used for separate obstacles.

- Each row in the experimenting record represents one experiment.

- The form has a "prediction side" (on the left) and an "evidence side" (on the right)

The information on the experimenting record is added by the learner before the next coaching cycle. During the coaching cycle the learner simply reads from this form in response to the coach's questions. The coach will either accept the learner's proposed next step (next experiment), or may give feedback to help improve the design of the next experiment.

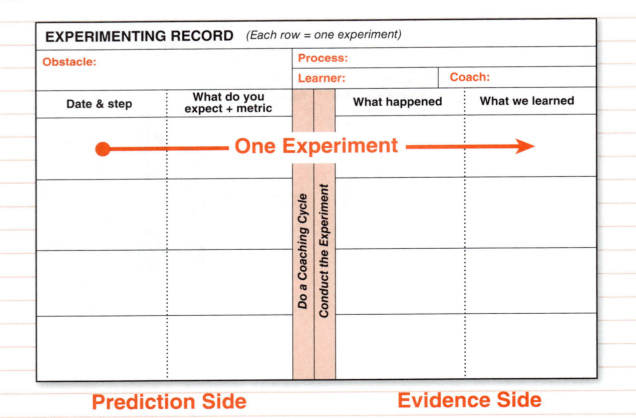

Source: *The Toyota Kata Practice Guide*

How the Learner Uses the Experimenting Record

EXPERIMENTING RECORD (Each row = one experiment)					
Obstacle:		**Process:**			
		Learner:		**Coach:**	
Date & step	**What do you expect + metric**	*Do a Coaching Cycle*	*Conduct the Experiment*	**What happened**	**What we learned**
1 ⟶	2 ⟶	3	4 ⟶	5 ⟶	6
7 ⟵	8				

1. Plan the experiment, indicating the proposed step and the date for that step.

2. Write down the effect you predict the step will have, or what you expect to learn, and how you will measure it.

3. **Go through a coaching cycle.** The coach gives feedback on the design of the next experiment as necessary. Make adjustments based on the coach's input.

4. Once you and the coach agree, conduct the experiment.

5. Record the facts and data about what actually happened. No interpretation yet!

6. Now reflect on the outcome of the experiment by comparing the predicted result (2) with what actually happened (5) and summarize what you learned.

7. Move down a row. Based on what you learned, propose the next step and date.

8. Write down your next prediction and how you will measure it.

Now it's time for the **next coaching cycle**.

Source: The Toyota Kata Practice Guide

COACHING KATA

The Five Questions

1. What is the **Target Condition**?
2. What is the **Actual Condition** now?

--------(Turn Card Over)-------------→

3. What **Obstacles** do you think are preventing you from reaching the target condition? Which *one* are you addressing now?
4. What is your **Next Step**? (Next experiment) What do you expect?
5. How quickly can we go and see what we **Have Learned** from taking that step?

*You'll often work on the same obstacle with several experiments

Steve

Process Steps Analysis						
Process: Gear Machining Changeover			**Learner:** Roger			
			Current Condition Date: May 24		**Target Condition** Date: June 15	
No.	**Process step**	**Observations**	Cum.	Step	Cum.	Step
			20´	20´	20´	20´
1	Drain machine		28´	8´	28´	8´
2	Lockout		35´	7´	35´	7´
3	Remove the tool		50´	15´	40´	5´
4	Install new tool		60´	10´	42´	2´
5	Adjust tool		63´	3´	45´	3´
6	Run test parts		72´	9´	54´	9´
7	Quality approval					
			72´		54´	

Obstacle Parking Lot

- Tool is heavy and difficult to handle
- Six different threaded fasteners
- Adjustment seems to be by personal experience
-
-
-
-

Roger

After reflecting on the last experiment, the next part of the coaching cycle can begin: discussing the next experiment!

Roger has already identified some obstacles that may need to be addressed, which are recorded in the *obstacles parking lot* in the lower right-hand corner of the learner's storyboard. This parking lot is simply a place to hold perceived obstacles, each of which may or may not end up getting addressed, while the learner works on one obstacle at a time.

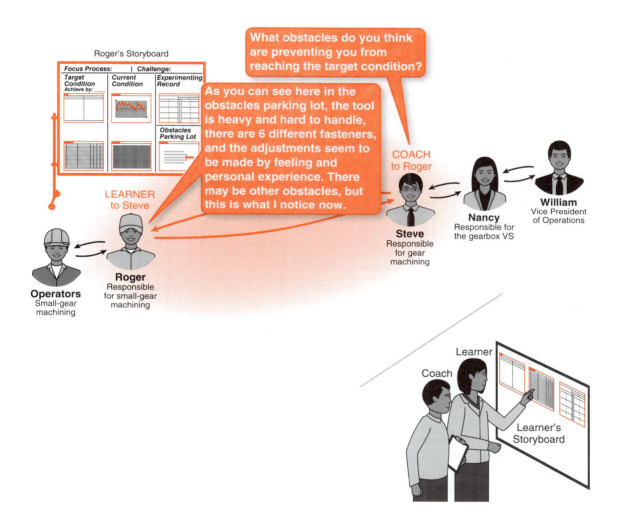

The Five Questions

① What is the **Target Condition**?

② What is the **Actual Condition** now?

--------(*Turn Card Over*)------------->

③ What **Obstacles** do you think are preventing you from reaching the target condition?
Which *one* are you addressing now?

④ What is your **Next Step**? (Next experiment) What do you expect?

⑤ How quickly can we go and see what we **Have Learned** from taking that step?

*You'll often work on the same obstacle with several experiments

COACHING KATA

Steve

Process Steps Analysis	Process: Gear Machining Changeover		Learner: Roger		Target Condition Date: June 15	
			Current Condition Date: May 24			
No.	Process step	Observations	Cum.	Step	Cum.	Step
			20´	20´	20´	20´
1	Drain machine		28´	8´	28´	8´
2	Lockout		35´	7´	35´	7´
3	Remove the tool		50´	15´	40´	5´
4	Install new tool		60´	10´	42´	2´
5	Adjust tool		63´	3´	45´	3´
6	Run test parts		72´	9´	54´	9´
7	Quality approval					
			72´		54´	

Roger

Obstacle Parking Lot

Current ➤

- Tool is heavy and difficult to handle
- Six different threaded fasteners
- Adjustment seems to be by personal experience
-
-
-
-
-
-
-
-

Roger focuses on one obstacle at a time, which he indicates with an arrow in the obstacles parking lot. His next experiments are done against that one indicated obstacle.

Important!

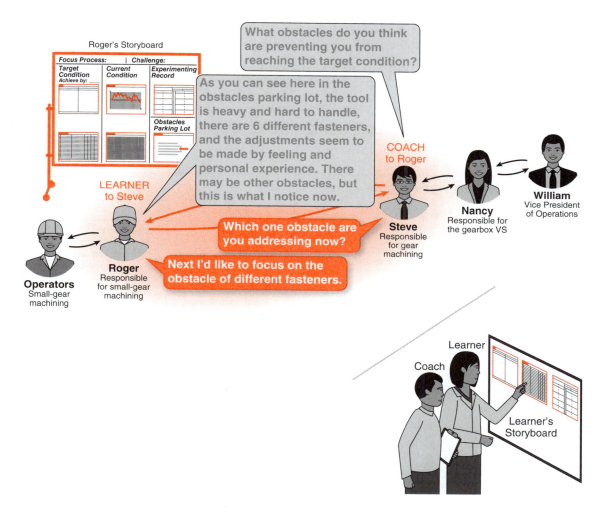

COACHING KATA

The Five Questions

① What is the **Target Condition**?

② What is the **Actual Condition** now?

--------(Turn Card Over)-------------->

③ What **Obstacles** do you think are preventing you from reaching the target condition?
Which *one* are you addressing now?

④ What is your **Next Step**? (Next experiment)
What do you expect?

⑤ How quickly can we go and see what we **Have Learned** from taking that step?

*You'll often work on the same obstacle with several experiments

Steve

EXPERIMENTING RECORD *(Each row = one experiment)*

Obstacle: *Six different threaded fasteners*

Process: *Changeover*

Learner: *Roger*   **Coach:** *Steve*

Date & step	What do you expect + metric	Do a Coaching Cycle	Conduct the Experiment	What happened	What we learned
Observe the changeover process and measure the time each step takes.	Understanding of steps, sequence, times and total time.			See process analysis sheet.	Process has 7 steps. Times for each step add up to 72 minutes.
By 3 p.m. today: Standardize fasteners to one size. Do new changeover, measure 7 steps.	Removing & installing tool takes 5 min less (10 min instead of 15 min).				

Roger

82

For an experiment to be scientific, the learner's prediction needs to be refutable, which also means it must be measureable in some way.

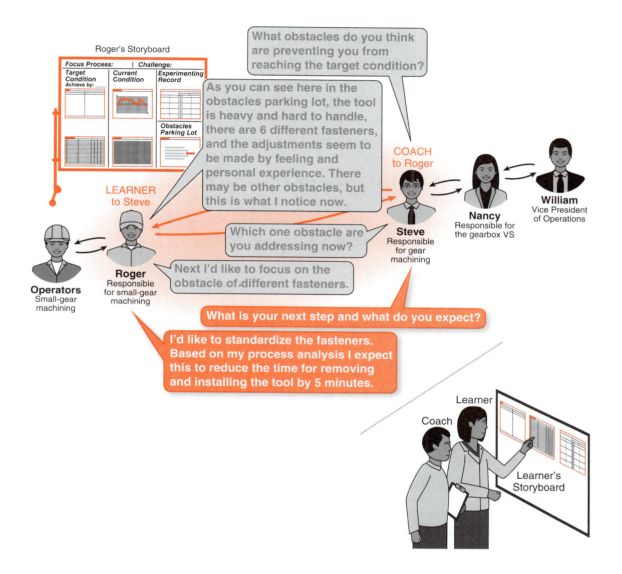

The Five Questions

① What is the **Target Condition**?

② What is the **Actual Condition** now?

--------(Turn Card Over)------------->

③ What **Obstacles** do you think are preventing you from reaching the target condition?
Which *one* are you addressing now?

④ What is your **Next Step**? (Next experiment)
What do you expect?

⑤ How quickly can we go and see what we **Have Learned** from taking that step?

*You'll often work on the same obstacle with several experiments

COACHING KATA

Steve

EXPERIMENTING RECORD   (Each row = one experiment)

Obstacle: *Six different threaded fasteners*		Process: *Changeover*		
		Learner: *Roger*		Coach: *Steve*
Date & step	**What do you expect + metric**		**What happened**	**What we learned**
Observe the changeover process and measure the time each step takes.	Understanding of steps, sequence, times and total time.	Do a Coaching Cycle — Conduct the Experiment	See process analysis sheet.	Process has 7 steps. Times for each step add up to 72 minutes.
By 3 p.m. today: Standardize fasteners to one size. Do new changeover, measure 7 steps.	Removing & installing tool takes 5 min less (10 min instead of 15 min).			

Then the time for Roger and Steve's next coaching cycle is confirmed.

Roger's Storyboard

How quickly can we go and see what we have learned from taking that step?

COACH to Roger

I think we don't need to wait until our next scheduled coaching cycle tomorrow, we could meet today at 3 PM if possible.

LEARNER to Steve

Nancy
Responsible for the gearbox VS

William
Vice President of Operations

Steve
Responsible for gear machining

OK, I'll be here at 3 PM. I'm curious to see what you've learned.

Roger
Responsible for small-gear machining

Operators
Small-gear machining

This Coaching Cycle is Done!

An important point to realize is that, as soon as the learner's next step is clear, the coaching cycle is essentially done. Other than confirming the time for the next coaching cycle, there is no need to discuss further because both coach and learner are now at a *knowledge threshold* and will only see further through the results of the learner's next experiment.

At the beginning this may be uncomfortable for managers who are accustomed to full action item lists. It may seem like such small steps will be too slow, but if you are experimenting every day, taking small steps will actually be faster and more effective than trying to know the exact path in advance.

After the Coaching Cycle: Feedback from Second Coach to Coach

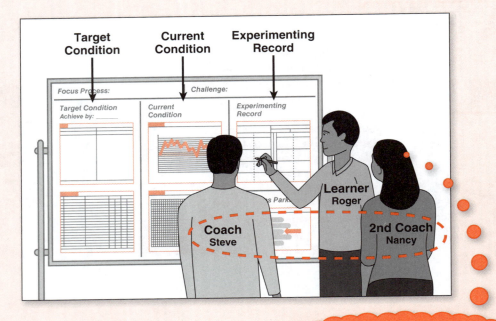

Now the Second Coach Gives Feedback to the Coach

Immediately after Roger and Steve's coaching cycle, Nancy gives Steve focused feedback on his latest coaching. She periodically watches Steve's coaching cycles for this purpose—not to audit or police Steve, but to give him specific, useful feedback for his own practice. (Note that some coaches prefer to get this feedback alone, while others like to have their learners there. It's up to you.)

The focus in this dialogue is on Steve's coaching practice. This feedback is normally focused on just one or two specific coaching points that Steve should work on practicing next.

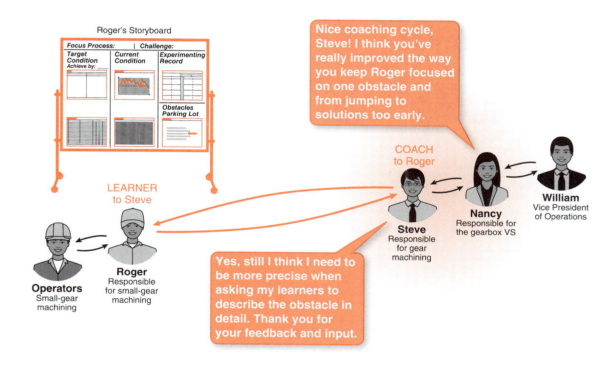

Summary So Far—Executing Phase

You have now seen the fundamental patterns of the Improvement Kata and Coaching Kata in action, in both the planning phase and the executing phase. Keep in mind that we are illustrating something that is already in place and running at Acme Gearbox Company, which you might view as a challenge to strive for. It takes practice to reach this level of competence in an organization.

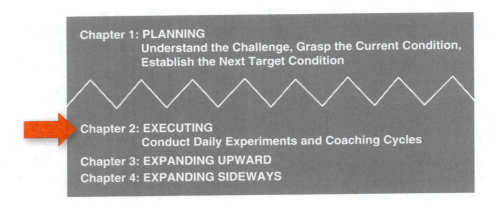

CHAPTER 3

EXPANDING UPWARD

About the Expanding Upward Chapter

The Improvement Kata and Coaching Kata Are Scalable Approaches for Managing an Improving, Adapting, Innovating Organization

The roles of learner and coach repeat as you move up the organization, with each coach in turn becoming a learner. This creates a routine of exchange, both up and down the hierarchy, that has several purposes:

- It develops everyone's Improvement Kata and Coaching Kata skills, through coached practice on real things. You're trying to build and maintain habits of scientific thinking at all levels. The more you can do that, the more power your organization has.

- It communicates up the hierarchy what is being learned about the organization's goals and the process of striving for them. This information can be used by Nancy and other higher-level managers to make adjustments in both strategy and tactics, based on facts and data gained from actual experiments.

- It gives the organization's leaders an ongoing sense of the level of improvement capability that exists in the organization. This is important in formulating new organization-level challenges, and for targeting skillsets to be developed.

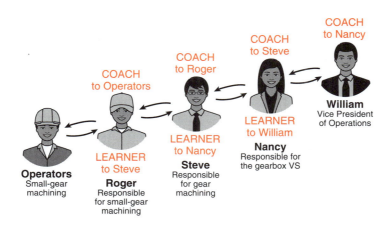

The Improvement Kata and Coaching Kata Become Fractal and Nested

Both the IK and CK patterns are fractal and repeat at every level of the organization. As we mentioned earlier, a *fractal* is something that has the same or a similar pattern at each scale level. Fractals are created by repeating a pattern over and over in a connected loop.

In our Acme case example, the coaching cycles continue from this point, but with a role change. Second coach Nancy shifts her role to first coach, and Steve shifts from first coach to Nancy's learner. This happens for two reasons:

- To communicate up the hierarchy what is being learned about the organization's goals and the process of striving for them. Going forward, this information can be used by Nancy and the managers above her, to assist in improving both of these aspects.

- To keep developing Steve's Improvement Kata skills. The learner at this level (Steve) also works on an obstacle of his own, applying the Improvement Kata pattern, which allows his coach (Nancy) to see which skills he needs to work on.

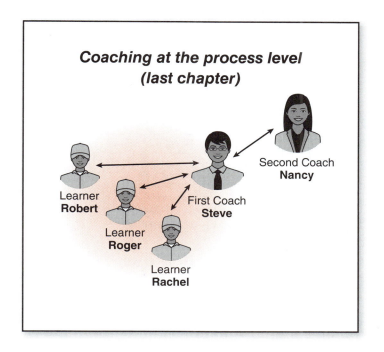

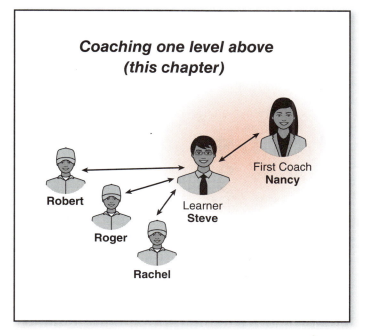

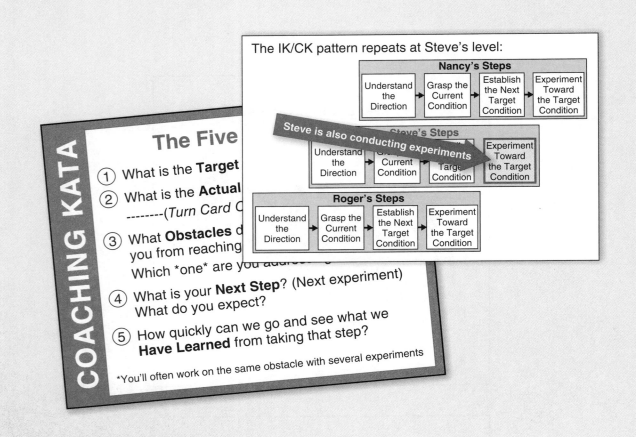

The IK/CK pattern repeats at Steve's level:

Nancy's Steps

| Understand the Direction | Grasp the Current Condition | Establish the Next Target Condition | Experiment Toward the Target Condition |

Steve's Steps

Steve is also conducting experiments

| Understand the Direction | Grasp the Current Condition | Target Condition | Experiment Toward the Target Condition |

Roger's Steps

| Understand the Direction | Grasp the Current Condition | Establish the Next Target Condition | Experiment Toward the Target Condition |

COACHING KATA

The Five

① What is the **Target**

② What is the **Actual**
--------(*Turn Card*

③ What **Obstacles** d
you from reaching
Which *one* are yo

④ What is your **Next Step**? (Next experiment)
What do you expect?

⑤ How quickly can we go and see what we
Have Learned from taking that step?

*You'll often work on the same obstacle with several experiments

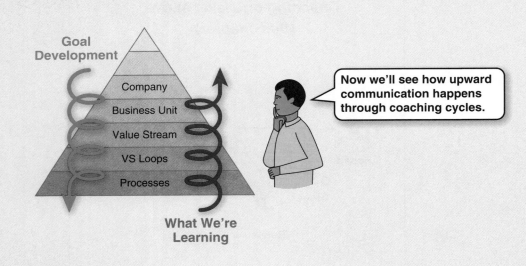

Goal
Development

Company

Business Unit

Value Stream

VS Loops

Processes

What We're
Learning

Now we'll see how upward
communication happens
through coaching cycles.

One Level Up, Nancy and Steve Also Meet Daily for Their Coaching Cycle

After Steve has coached his learners, Nancy meets with him for a daily coaching cycle at the value stream loop level. This coaching cycle follows the same pattern of the five Coaching Kata questions, which are the main headings.

This coaching is related to *Steve's* target condition and the learnings he and his learners are acquiring as they experiment toward their next target conditions. After these coaching cycles, Nancy may update her value stream map, by adding things she has learned.

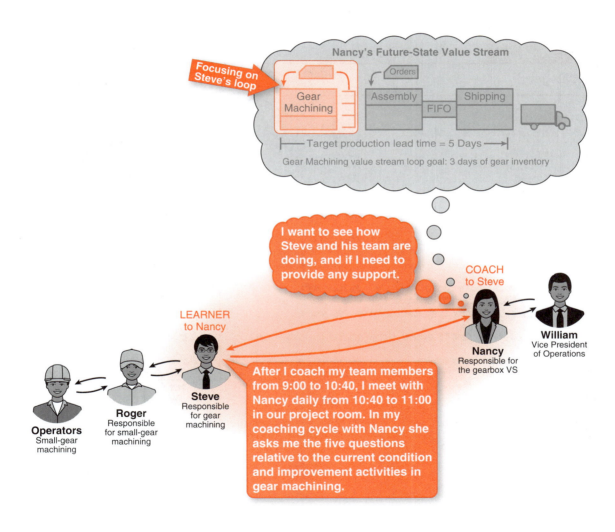

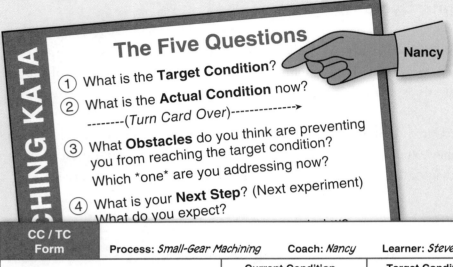

The Five Questions

① What is the **Target Condition**?

② What is the **Actual Condition** now?

--------(Turn Card Over)-------------->

③ What **Obstacles** do you think are preventing you from reaching the target condition? Which *one* are you addressing now?

④ What is your **Next Step**? (Next experiment) What do you expect?

Nancy

CC / TC Form	Process: *Small-Gear Machining*	Coach: *Nancy*	Learner: *Steve*

Category	Current Condition May 17	Target Condition August 25	
Stock	30 days	3 days	Steve's target condition
Safety factor		1 day	
EPEI (time to cycle through all parts)		2 days	
Total types	30	40 types	
Runners	8 typ	12 types	
Specials	22 types (2/20 days)	28 types (4/2 days)	
Total types every EPEI	10 types every 20 days	16 types every 2 days	
Changeovers required every day	0.5 (1 every 2 days)	8 changeovers/day	
Time available every day	1,320 minutes	1,320 minutes	
Minus unplanned downtime	-20% = 1,056 min total available	-15% = 1,122 min total available	
Time required for running			
Total pieces required per month	10,200/month	12,120/month	
Total pieces per day (20 days/month)	510/day	606/day	
Planned run time (pl. cycle time)/item	120 seconds	100 seconds	
Run time required/day (p/CT x pieces)	61,200 sec = 1,020 min	60,600 sec = 1,010 min	
Time available/day for changeovers	1,056 total minutes -1,020 min for run ——————— 36 min for all changeovers	1,122 total minutes - 1,010 min for run ——————— 112 min for all changeovers	
Divided by changeovers required/day	36/0.5 = 72 min/changeover	112/8 = 14 min/changeover	
Summary of Target Condition			
Cycle time per piece	120 seconds	100 seconds	← Robert's challenge
Unplanned downtime	20 %	15 %	← Rachel's challenge
Changeover time	72 minutes	14 minutes	← Roger's challenge

Steve

Nancy Begins with the First of the Five Coaching Kata Questions

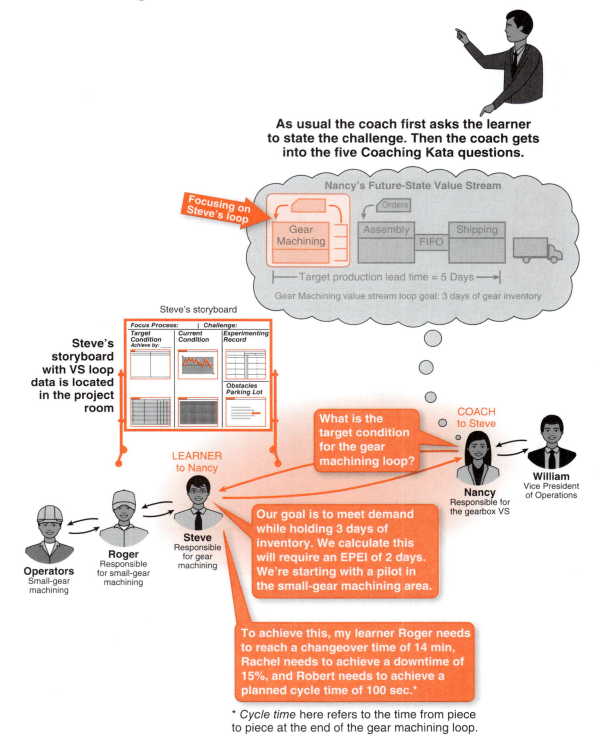

As usual the coach first asks the learner to state the challenge. Then the coach gets into the five Coaching Kata questions.

Nancy's Future-State Value Stream

Focusing on Steve's loop

Orders

Gear Machining

Assembly — FIFO — Shipping

Target production lead time = 5 Days

Gear Machining value stream loop goal: 3 days of gear inventory

Steve's storyboard

Steve's storyboard with VS loop data is located in the project room

Focus Process: | Challenge:

Target Condition Achieve by: ___ | Current Condition | Experimenting Record

Obstacles Parking Lot

COACH to Steve

What is the target condition for the gear machining loop?

Nancy Responsible for the gearbox VS

William Vice President of Operations

LEARNER to Nancy

Steve Responsible for gear machining

Our goal is to meet demand while holding 3 days of inventory. We calculate this will require an EPEI of 2 days. We're starting with a pilot in the small-gear machining area.

Operators Small-gear machining

Roger Responsible for small-gear machining

To achieve this, my learner Roger needs to reach a changeover time of 14 min, Rachel needs to achieve a downtime of 15%, and Robert needs to achieve a planned cycle time of 100 sec.*

* *Cycle time* here refers to the time from piece to piece at the end of the gear machining loop.

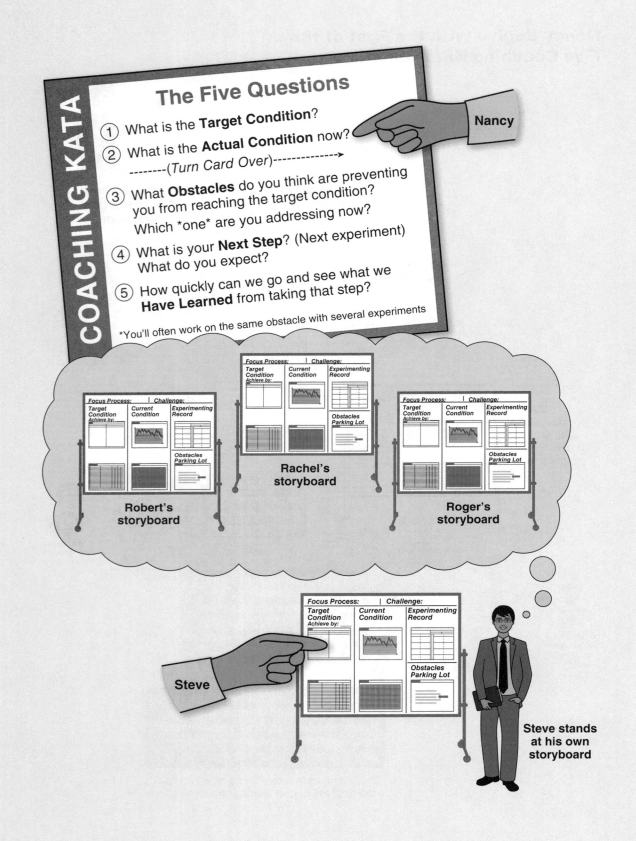

Steve's Answers Are Based on Information from His Learners' Storyboards

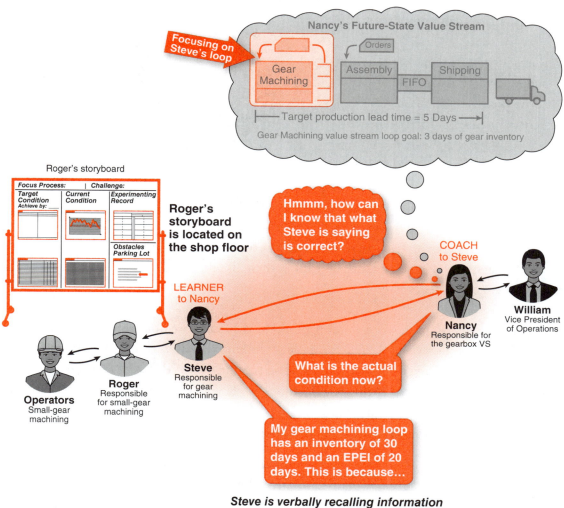

Steve is verbally recalling information that is found on Roger, Rachel, and Robert's storyboards.

Nancy Has a Problem!

WARNING!

Expanding up the chain includes communicating information that originates from learners at the process level. Unfortunately, we cannot rely on our faulty human memory for this communication.

Perhaps ideally, in their value stream–level coaching cycles, Nancy and Steve would visit the boards of all of Steve's learners, which are located at their respective processes. That way, both Nancy and Steve would have a good grasp of the actual condition based on the facts and data posted there.

> Hmmm, how can I know that what Steve is saying is correct?

Nancy
Responsible for the gearbox VS

However, Nancy has four learners who each in turn have multiple learners, and each of Nancy's coaching cycles should not take more than 20 minutes. There are a variety of ways this problem can be addressed:

Go and See

- Perhaps, in your organization, the distances are not great and you can in fact visit all the relevant learner storyboards within one 20-minute coaching cycle. Or you might select one or two different learner storyboards to go see each time. While you are there you can also see each focus process firsthand, which is always a good thing. However, in many organizations this will not be possible, or not possible every time.

Notebook

- Another option is that the learner (Steve, in this case) keeps a notebook of information obtained in the earlier coaching cycles with his learners, from which he reads during the coaching cycle with his coach (Nancy). However, keeping such a notebook is still subject to Steve's interpretation of the facts.

Board

- A coaching summary board that the learner (here, Steve) updates before his coaching cycle (here, with Nancy). These boards are often located in a project room or "war room," which the Lean community sometimes calls "Obeya."

Example Solution: A Coaching Summary Board

This is one way to keep your higher-level coaching cycles grounded in facts and data, and consolidate information for effective communication.

Immediately after each coaching cycle with his learners, Steve fills out a coaching summary card to capture the learnings recorded in their experimenting records. The information on the coaching summary card follows the pattern of the five Coaching Kata questions. This makes reporting upward the same basic routine at all levels, which makes this process go quickly. Steve places these cards on the coaching summary board in the project room, before his coaching cycle with Nancy. He uses a green card to indicate "on schedule, we don't need support" or a red card to indicate "this learner is behind schedule" or even "this coach/learner pair needs support from the second coach." In this last instance, the coach is escalating the problem and will ask for support from their next-level coach.

Coaching Summary Cards

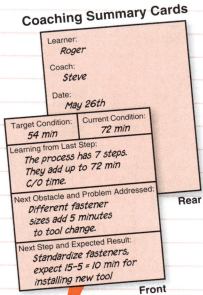

This procedure repeats at every level, for example with Nancy in preparation for her coaching cycle with her boss, William. The summary board and coaching summary cards are used by all coaches to communicate upward at all levels.

A coaching summary board can be several feet wide and might look like this (*below*). There may even be more than one coaching summary board along a value stream, depending on the size and/or location of the teams in the value stream.

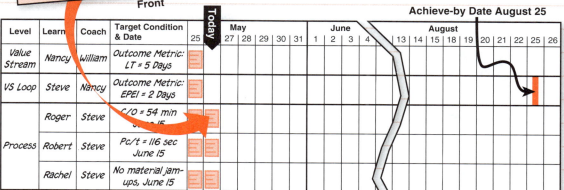

99

COACHING KATA

The Five Questions

Nancy

① What is the **Target Condition**?

② What is the **Actual Condition** now?

--------(*Turn Card Over*)------------->

③ What **Obstacles** do you think are preventing you from reaching the target condition? Which *one* are you addressing now?

④ What is your **Next Step**? (Next experiment) What do you expect?

⑤ How quickly can we go and see what we **Have Learned** from taking that step?

*You'll often work on the same obstacle with several experiments

Level	Learner	Coach	Target Condition & Date	May 25	26	27	28
Value Stream	Nancy	William	Outcome Metric: Lead Time = 5 Days	▭			
VS Loop	Steve	Nancy	Outcome Metric: EPEI = 2 Days	▭			
Process	Robert	Steve	C/O = 54 min June 15	▭	▭		
	Robert	Steve	Pc/t = 116 sec June 15	▭	▭		
	Rachel	Steve	No material jam-ups, June 15	▭	▭		

Steve

Coaching Summary Board

Let's Start Over, but This Time with Steve Using a Coaching Summary Board and Cards

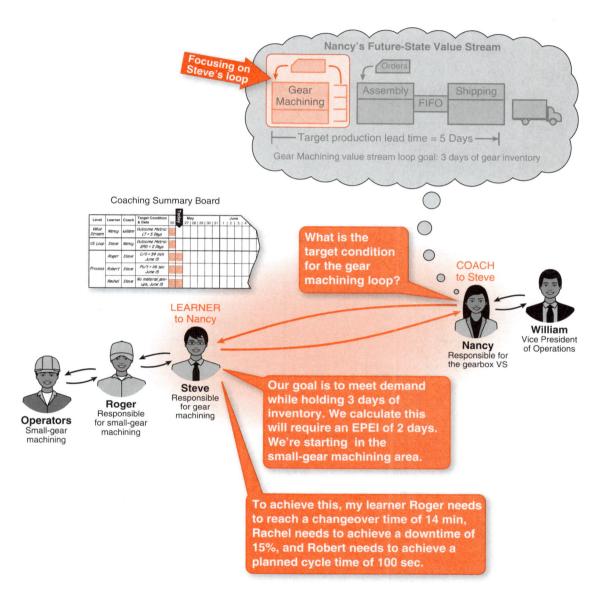

Steve is pointing at coaching summary cards.

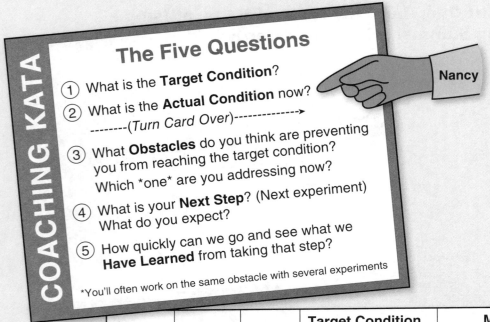

The Five Questions

COACHING KATA

① What is the **Target Condition**?

② What is the **Actual Condition** now?

-------(Turn Card Over)-------→

③ What **Obstacles** do you think are preventing you from reaching the target condition? Which *one* are you addressing now?

④ What is your **Next Step**? (Next experiment) What do you expect?

⑤ How quickly can we go and see what we **Have Learned** from taking that step?

*You'll often work on the same obstacle with several experiments

Nancy

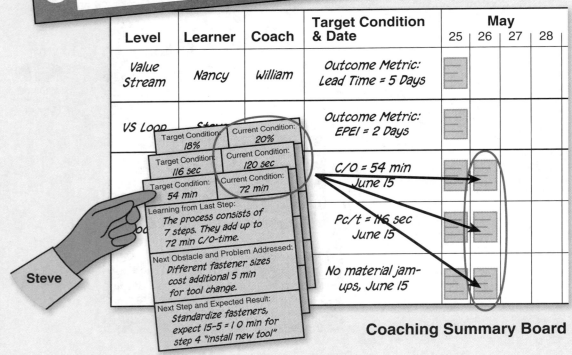

Level	Learner	Coach	Target Condition & Date	May 25	26	27	28
Value Stream	Nancy	William	Outcome Metric: Lead Time = 5 Days				
VS Loop	Steve		Outcome Metric: EPEI = 2 Days				
			C/O = 54 min June 15				
			Pc/t = 116 sec June 15				
			No material jam-ups, June 15				

Target Condition: 18%

Current Condition: 20%

Target Condition: 116 sec

Current Condition: 120 sec

Target Condition: 54 min

Current Condition: 72 min

Learning from Last Step: The process consists of 7 steps. They add up to 72 min C/O-time.

Next Obstacle and Problem Addressed: Different fastener sizes cost additional 5 min for tool change.

Next Step and Expected Result: Standardize fasteners, expect 15-5 = 10 min for step 4 "install new tool"

Steve

Coaching Summary Board

Now Steve's Answers Are Based on Information from the Coaching Summary Cards

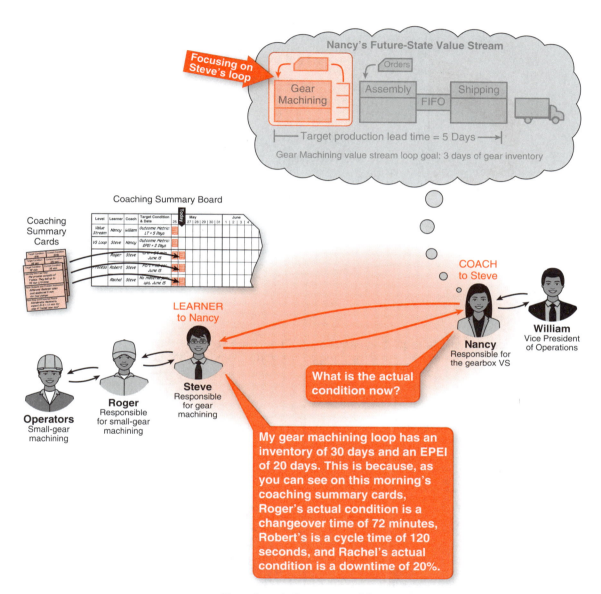

Steve is pointing at coaching summary cards.

**The coach flips the five question card over,
to the reflection section on the back.**

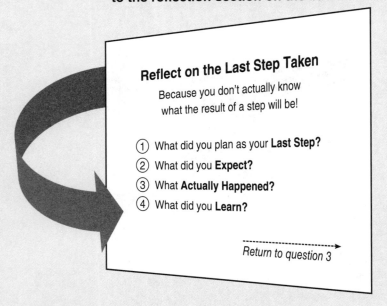

Reflect on the Last Step Taken

Because you don't actually know
what the result of a step will be!

① What did you plan as your **Last Step?**

② What did you **Expect?**

③ What **Actually Happened?**

④ What did you **Learn?**

- - - - - - - - - - - - - - - →
Return to question 3

The three reflections regarding Steve's learners are done first, by Steve reading the coaching summary cards. The learners are not present in this coaching cycle.

Then Steve's own reflection is done, using his storyboard.

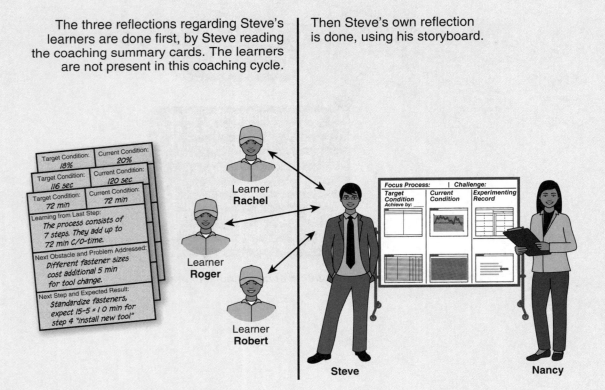

Now Nancy Asks About Steve's Learners' Experiments

Nancy does this once for each of Steve's learners (using the respective coaching summary cards), and then once for Steve's experiments.

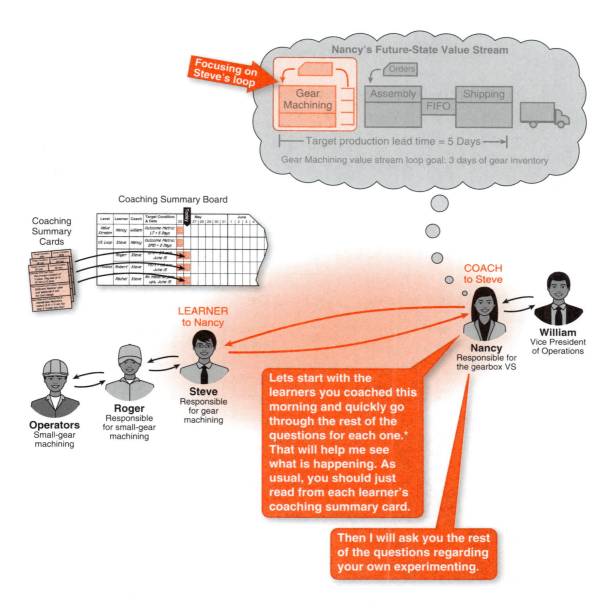

* In this example we are only going to look at Roger.

The coach now uses the reflection section on the back of the card.

Reflect on the Last Step Taken

Because you don't actually know
what the result of a step will be!

① What did you plan as your **Last Step?**

② What did you **Expect?**

③ What **Actually Happened?**

④ What did you **Learn?**

------------------------------->
Return to question 3

Nancy

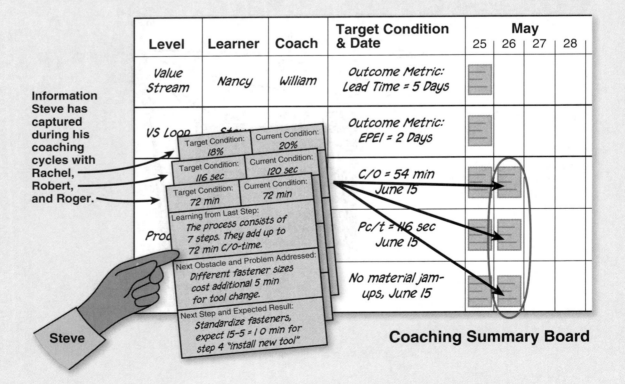

Information Steve has captured during his coaching cycles with Rachel, Robert, and Roger.

Level	Learner	Coach	Target Condition & Date	May			
				25	26	27	28
Value Stream	Nancy	William	Outcome Metric: Lead Time = 5 Days	▭			
VS Loop	Steve		Outcome Metric: EPEI = 2 Days	▭			
			C/O = 54 min June 15	▭	▭		
Proc			Pc/t = 116 sec June 15	▭	▭		
			No material jam-ups, June 15	▭	▭		

Target Condition: 18%   Current Condition: 20%

Target Condition: 116 sec   Current Condition: 120 sec

Target Condition: 72 min   Current Condition: 72 min

Learning from Last Step:
The process consists of 7 steps. They add up to 72 min C/O-time.

Next Obstacle and Problem Addressed:
Different fastener sizes cost additional 5 min for tool change.

Next Step and Expected Result:
Standardize fasteners, expect 15–5 = 10 min for step 4 "install new tool"

Steve

Coaching Summary Board

First, Nancy Asks the Reflection Questions for Each of Steve's Learners *(In This Example, Only Roger)*

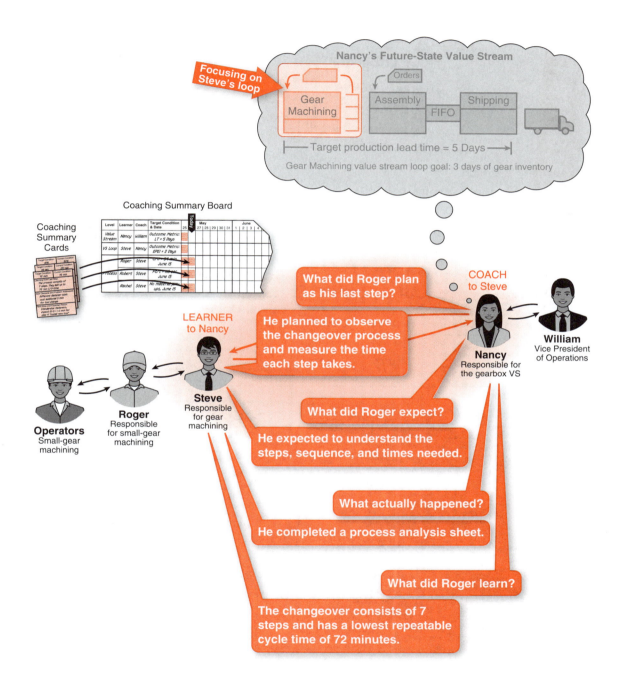

The coach flips the five question card to the front

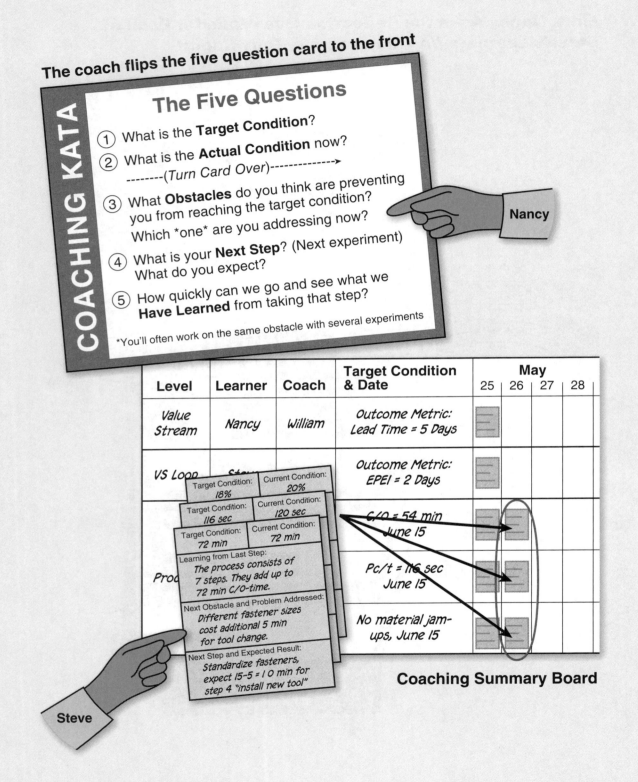

COACHING KATA

The Five Questions

(1) What is the **Target Condition**?

(2) What is the **Actual Condition** now?
--------(Turn Card Over)-------------->

(3) What **Obstacles** do you think are preventing you from reaching the target condition? Which *one* are you addressing now?

(4) What is your **Next Step**? (Next experiment) What do you expect?

(5) How quickly can we go and see what we **Have Learned** from taking that step?

*You'll often work on the same obstacle with several experiments

Nancy

Level	Learner	Coach	Target Condition & Date	May			
				25	26	27	28
Value Stream	Nancy	William	Outcome Metric: Lead Time = 5 Days				
VS Loop	Steve		Outcome Metric: EPEI = 2 Days				
Proc			C/O = 54 min June 15				
			Pc/t = 116 sec June 15				
			No material jam-ups, June 15				

Target Condition: 18%   Current Condition: 20%

Target Condition: 116 sec   Current Condition: 120 sec

Target Condition: 72 min   Current Condition: 72 min

Learning from Last Step:
The process consists of 7 steps. They add up to 72 min C/o-time.

Next Obstacle and Problem Addressed:
Different fastener sizes cost additional 5 min for tool change.

Next Step and Expected Result:
Standardize fasteners, expect 15-5 = 10 min for step 4 "install new tool"

Steve

Coaching Summary Board

Then, Nancy Asks About the Next Steps of Each of Steve's Learners (*In This Example, Only Roger*)

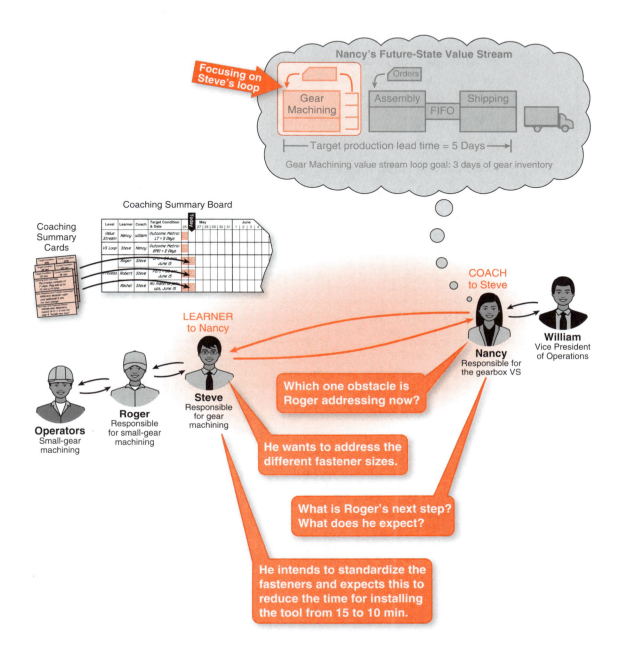

Back of the five question card (reflection section)

Reflect on the Last Step Taken

Because you don't actually know
what the result of a step will be!

1. What did you plan as your **Last Step?**
2. What did you **Expect?**
3. What **Actually Happened?**
4. What did you **Learn?**

Nancy

-------------------------------->
Return to question 3

EXPERIMENTING RECORD (Each row = one experiment)

Obstacle: *Organization's constraints block improvement work.*		Process: *Gear Machining*		
		Learner: *Steve*		Coach: *Nancy*
Date & step	**What do you expect + metric**		**What happened**	**What we learned**
On May 25th rearrange production plan.	*Allow for 2 hours of time for Roger to do changeover experiments.*		*Overtime was accorded, additional machine was activated.*	*4 hours of time could be made available to Roger instead of the expected 2 hours.*
May 26th: Assist Rachel with downtime analysis.	*Understand pattern & sources of downtime*			

Do a Coaching Cycle

Conduct the Experiment

Steve

Nancy Shifts to Steve and Does a Reflection with Him

After having learned about the status of Steve's three learners' improvement efforts, Nancy and Steve move to Steve's storyboard, which is also located close to the coaching summary board in the war room. There, Steve refers to his own experimenting record to explain to Nancy his learnings and next step.

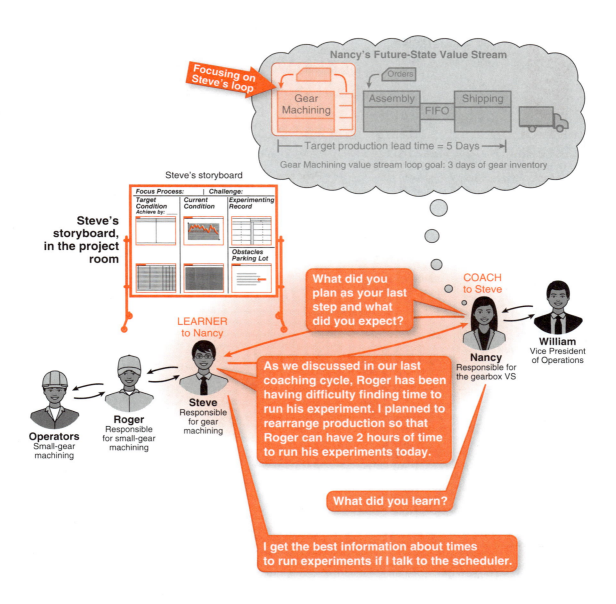

Front of the five question card

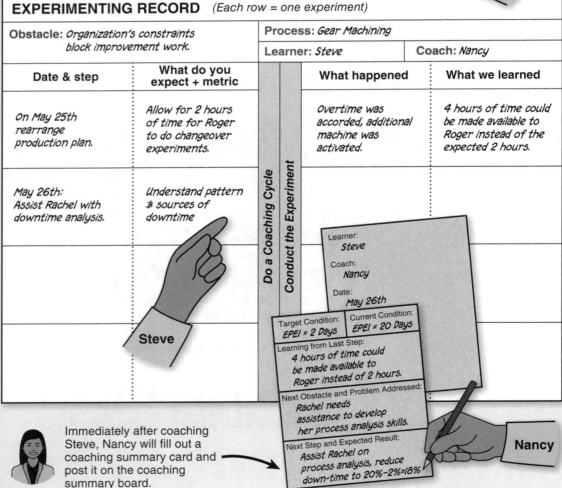

The Five Questions

COACHING KATA

① What is the **Target Condition**?

② What is the **Actual Condition** now?
-------(Turn Card Over)------------→

③ What **Obstacles** do you think are preventing you from reaching the target condition? Which *one* are you addressing now?

④ What is your **Next Step**? (Next experiment) What do you expect?

⑤ ~~How quickly~~ can we go and see what we

Nancy

EXPERIMENTING RECORD   (Each row = one experiment)

Obstacle: *Organization's constraints block improvement work.*		Process: *Gear Machining*	
		Learner: *Steve*	Coach: *Nancy*

Date & step	What do you expect + metric		What happened	What we learned
On May 25th rearrange production plan.	Allow for 2 hours of time for Roger to do changeover experiments.		Overtime was accorded, additional machine was activated.	4 hours of time could be made available to Roger instead of the expected 2 hours.
May 26th: Assist Rachel with downtime analysis.	Understand pattern & sources of downtime			

(vertical center column:) Do a Coaching Cycle — Conduct the Experiment

Steve

Learner:
Steve

Coach:
Nancy

Date:
May 26th

Target Condition: *EPEI = 2 Days*	Current Condition: *EPEI = 20 Days*

Learning from Last Step:
4 hours of time could be made available to Roger instead of 2 hours.

Next Obstacle and Problem Addressed:
Rachel needs assistance to develop her process analysis skills.

Next Step and Expected Result:
Assist Rachel on process analysis, reduce down-time to 20%-2%=18%

Nancy

Immediately after coaching Steve, Nancy will fill out a coaching summary card and post it on the coaching summary board.

Nancy Flips the Five Question Card to the Front to Coach Steve's Next Step

Nancy looks to confirm that Steve is using an experimenting record, since it is one of the learner's main Starter Kata for practicing scientific thinking.

Afterward, Steve leaves the room and Nancy stays to do her coaching cycle with her coach, William, who has just arrived. The same routine repeats one level up.

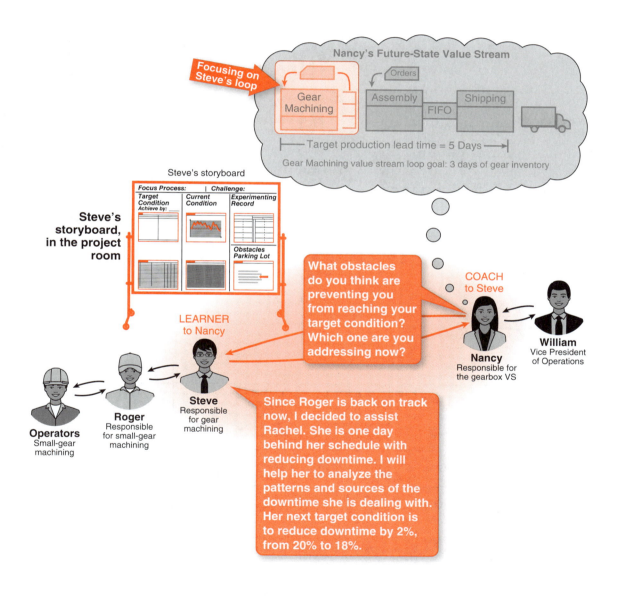

Summary So Far—Expanding Upward

The coaching chain gets completed and learnings are moving upward. Coaching cycles repeat across each level of the organization, as shown below. Process-level coaching cycles took place at the learner storyboards, near each learner's focus process. Above that level, the coaching cycles took place at a coaching summary board.

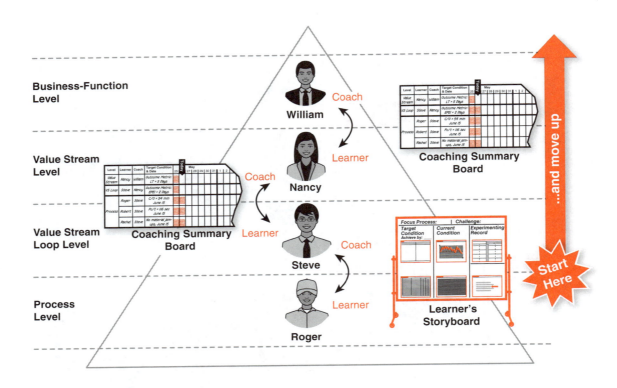

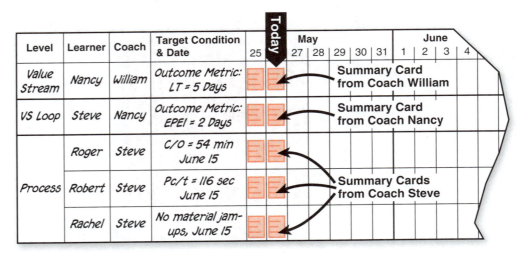

Level	Learner	Coach	Target Condition & Date	25	Today	May 27	28	29	30	31	June 1	2	3	4	
Value Stream	Nancy	William	Outcome Metric: LT = 5 Days								Summary Card from Coach William				
VS Loop	Steve	Nancy	Outcome Metric: EPEI = 2 Days								Summary Card from Coach Nancy				
Process	Roger	Steve	C/O = 54 min June 15												
	Robert	Steve	Pc/t = 116 sec June 15								Summary Cards from Coach Steve				
	Rachel	Steve	No material jam-ups, June 15												

At this point, you have seen the fundamental patterns of the Improvement Kata and Coaching Kata get repeated both up and down the organization, to align and connect the levels of the organization.

Distributing a strategic challenge down into an organization, whose individual teams practice a scientific way of navigating toward goals, is part of the picture. However, the upward flow of information that you just saw is an equally vital element of a policy deployment system, because that is where an adaptiveness, built on learnings from incrementally unfolding reality, comes from.

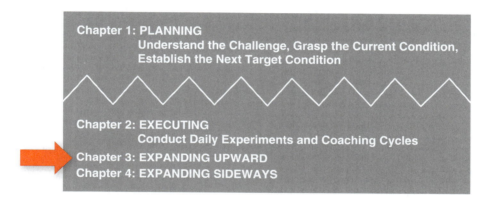

CHAPTER 4

EXPANDING SIDEWAYS

Handling Obstacles at Interfaces

About the Expanding Sideways Chapter

Using the Improvement Kata and Coaching Kata to Handle Obstacles at the Interfaces and Coordinate Improvement Teams

At this point we've painted a picture of top-to-bottom-and-back-again structure and routines for practicing scientific skills in order to meet challenging goals. However, don't let the clarity of that picture fool you into believing that it's a straightforward process of *implementation* to complete such a structure. There will always be problems, both in your efforts to develop the skills and structure, and in your efforts to apply these skills and structure to your organization's goals.

Here's the positive side of that. The problems that arise along the way can also be useful, because they show you what you need to work on, i.e., where adjustments and course corrections are necessary. That is, as long as you have a means of becoming aware of problems quickly and reacting effectively.

Ideally problems are handled as close to the source as possible, and many problems can be taken care of directly by the learner and their coach within the framework of their daily coaching cycles. In fact, such close-to-the-source problem solving is one reason for conducting daily, one-on-one coaching cycles. But things can also get more complicated.

As your organization's improvement and coaching capabilities expand and multiple learners are being coached toward a shared challenge, an additional need to coordinate *teams* will naturally emerge. Luckily, you can use the same Coaching Kata pattern to coach for improved team communication and coordination.

Steve schedules his daily one-on-one coaching cycles early in the day.

Steve also schedules a daily group coaching cycle with all his learners and, as needed, his coach Nancy.

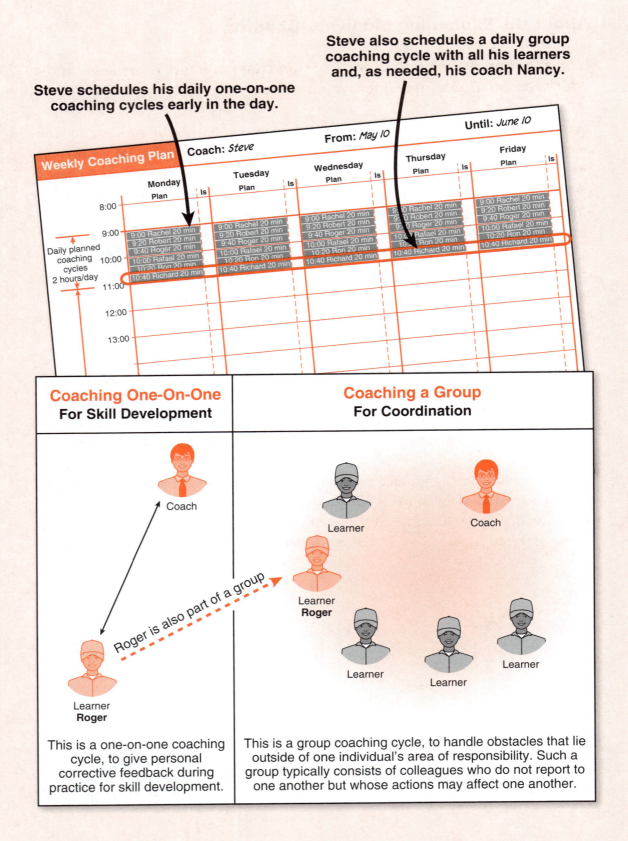

Weekly Coaching Plan
Coach: *Steve*   From: *May 10*   Until: *June 10*

	Monday Plan	Is	Tuesday Plan	Is	Wednesday Plan	Is	Thursday Plan	Is	Friday Plan	Is
8:00							9:00 Rachel 20 min 9:20 Robert 20 min 9:40 Roger 20 min		9:00 Rachel 20 min 9:20 Robert 20 min 9:40 Roger 20 min	
9:00	9:00 Rachel 20 min 9:20 Robert 20 min 9:40 Roger 20 min 10:00 Rafael 20 min		9:00 Rachel 20 min 9:20 Robert 20 min 9:40 Roger 20 min 10:00 Rafael 20 min		9:00 Rachel 20 min 9:40 Roger 20 min 10:00 Rafael 20 min		10:00 Rafael 20 min		10:00 Rafael 20 min	
10:00	10:20 Ron 20 min 10:40 Richard 20 min		10:20 Ron 20 min 10:40 Richard 20 min		10:20 Ron 20 min 10:40 Richard 20 min		10:20 Ron 20 min 10:40 Richard 20 min		10:20 Ron 20 min 10:40 Richard 20 min	
11:00										
12:00										
13:00										

Daily planned coaching cycles 2 hours/day

Coaching One-On-One
For Skill Development

Coach

Learner **Roger**

Roger is also part of a group

This is a one-on-one coaching cycle, to give personal corrective feedback during practice for skill development.

Coaching a Group
For Coordination

Learner

Coach

Learner **Roger**

Learner   Learner   Learner

This is a group coaching cycle, to handle obstacles that lie outside of one individual's area of responsibility. Such a group typically consists of colleagues who do not report to one another but whose actions may affect one another.

Handling Obstacles at Interfaces

At this point in the work day, the individual coaching cycles at the process level, as well as upward communication, have occurred. When working on a shared target condition, coordinating the activities of multiple learners or teams to address obstacles that lie beyond their area of control becomes an additional coaching task.

One way to do this is for each coach and all their learners to meet for a short group coaching cycle, typically once a day. This sort of group-coordination meeting is already a normal activity for most managers, but it is made more effective through practice of the Improvement Kata and Coaching Kata. A group coaching cycle is often done standing up, for instance at a coaching summary board where facts and data are summarized.

Some ways that obstacles at interfaces can come to the attention of a coach are:

1. A learner asks for cross-interface help.

2. The coach notices that cross-interface help is needed.

3. A problem is pointed out by another department or team.

On the next pages we give some examples and illustrate how group coaching helps you stay coordinated and meet target condition achieve-by dates.

Coaching Summary Board

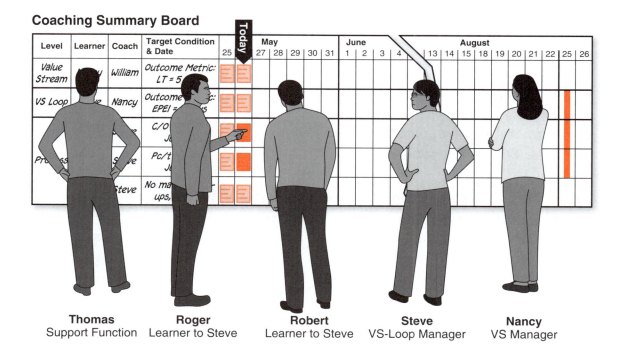

Thomas Support Function	**Roger** Learner to Steve	**Robert** Learner to Steve	**Steve** VS-Loop Manager	**Nancy** VS Manager

Why Conduct Group Coaching Cycles?

1. To Reveal Obstacles at the Interfaces

Some obstacles will have their origins outside the working scope of the learner, in the scope of another process. In addition, introducing changes and improvements in one part of a value stream can become the source of unexpected or unintended changes in another part of the value stream.

Such obstacles at the interfaces often remain hidden until they become a bigger problem. Group coaching cycles prevent this by providing a structured, scientific approach for communication and coordination between departments.

2. To Get Support Quickly

There are two basic reasons why learners may not be able to overcome an obstacle by themselves:

1. The learner is organizationally not able to do it, because the obstacle involves persons outside the learner's scope of responsibility.

2. The learner is technically not able to do it.

The coach decides what external support is necessary or what support to provide. Maybe the learner's capabilities can be developed to solve the problem themselves at the working level, and it may be appropriate to coach the learner through dealing with a cross-departmental issue themselves.

3. To Prevent a Learner's Steps from Producing Negative Effects Elsewhere

Since with policy deployment many team members are working on different aspects of the same challenge, everyone is potentially influencing everyone else's work. Ideally, coaches will even see and encourage dealing with coordination issues *before* a learner introduces a particular step.

Preventing Obstacles at Interfaces

Meeting target condition achieve-by dates becomes ever more important as improvement efforts involve more people and bigger challenges. One approach coaches can use to handle problems is to increase their coaching cycle frequency as and where needed, to get a learner back on track and prevent small time delays from growing into bigger ones that will affect others. When this is insufficient, the next step is to escalate the problem to the next-level coach for support.

Some example problem scenarios and coaching responses are shown on the coaching summary board below.

These blank spaces indicate that two coaching cycles between Roger and Steve didn't take place.
Nancy might ask, "What obstacles are currently keeping you from coaching your learner every day?"

A red card indicates that Steve and Nancy are behind schedule.
Nancy might seek support from her coach William.

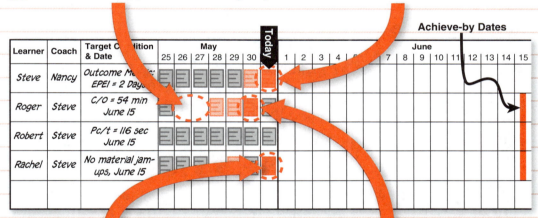

This red card indicates that Rachel and Steve are behind schedule.
When asked by Nancy, Rachel and Steve might say, "We can handle this ourselves."

This red card indicates that Roger and Steve are behind schedule.
Noticing three red cards in a row, Nancy might say, "Steve, I notice you have three red cards. I think you should increase your coaching frequency with Roger."

121

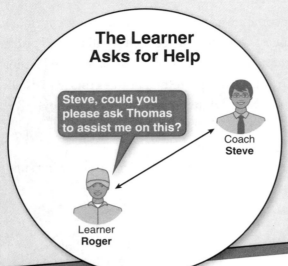

**The Learner
Asks for Help**

Steve, could you please ask Thomas to assist me on this?

Coach
Steve

Learner
Roger

COACHING KATA

The Five Questions

1. What is the **Target Condition**?

2. What is the **Actual Condition** now?

--------(*Turn Card Over*)------------->

3. What **Obstacles** do you think are preventing you from reaching the target condition? Which *one* are you addressing now?

4. What is your **Next Step**? (Next experiment) What do you expect?

5. How quickly can we go and see what we **Have Learned** from taking that step?

*You'll often work on the same obstacle with several experiments

Steve

Example 1: Roger Asks for Cross-Interface Help

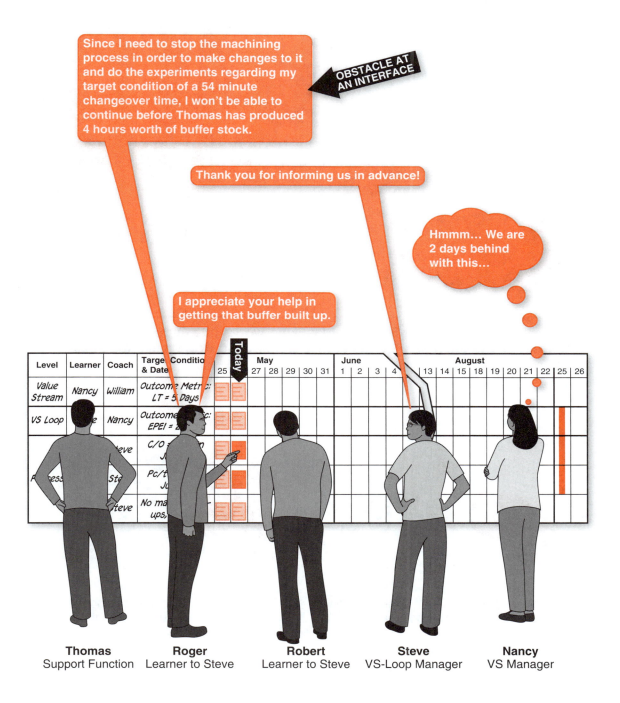

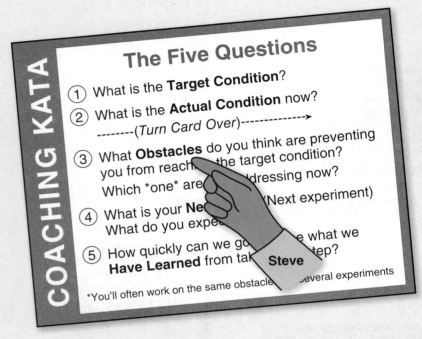

The Five Questions

① What is the **Target Condition**?

② What is the **Actual Condition** now?

--------(Turn Card Over)------------->

③ What **Obstacles** do you think are preventing you from reach___ the target condition?
Which *one* are ___ ___dressing now?

④ What is your Ne___ ___ (Next experiment)
What do you expe___ ___ ___

⑤ How quickly can we g___ ___ e what we
Have Learned from ta___ ___ tep?

*You'll often work on the same obstacle___ several experiments

COACHING KATA

Steve

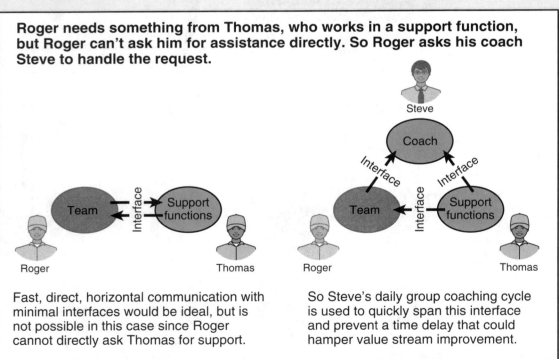

Roger needs something from Thomas, who works in a support function, but Roger can't ask him for assistance directly. So Roger asks his coach Steve to handle the request.

Steve

Coach

Interface   Interface

Team   Support functions

Interface

Roger   Thomas

Team   Interface   Support functions

Roger   Thomas

Fast, direct, horizontal communication with minimal interfaces would be ideal, but is not possible in this case since Roger cannot directly ask Thomas for support.

So Steve's daily group coaching cycle is used to quickly span this interface and prevent a time delay that could hamper value stream improvement.

Thomas, Roger, and Steve are all present in the group coaching cycle, so Thomas can answer the request for his support immediately. This is considerably more expedient than if Steve waited until his next one-on-one coaching cycle with Thomas the following day.

The more quickly an issue can be brought to the right person, the faster the obstacle can be addressed, and the less likely that elements of the value stream improvement effort will be delayed and disrupted.

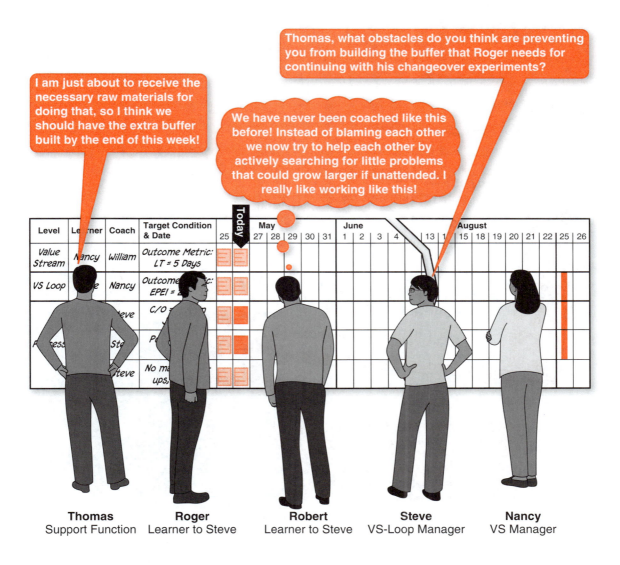

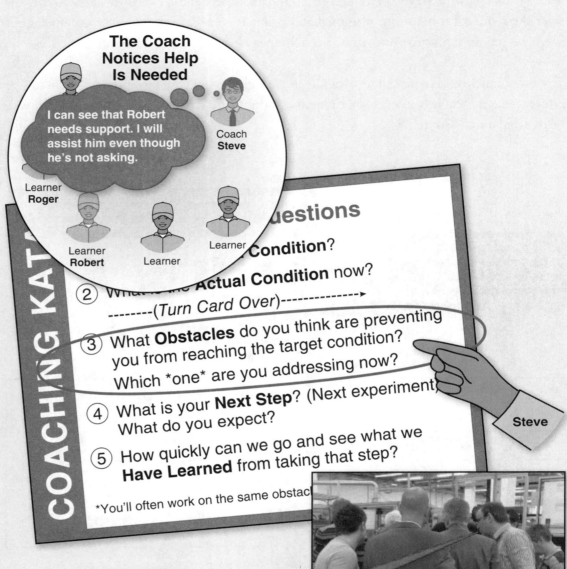

The Coach Notices Help Is Needed

I can see that Robert needs support. I will assist him even though he's not asking.

Coach **Steve**

Learner **Roger**

Learner **Robert**

Learner

Learner

COACHING KAT...

...uestions

... **Condition**?

② What ... **Actual Condition** now?

--------(Turn Card Over)-------------->

③ What **Obstacles** do you think are preventing you from reaching the target condition? Which *one* are you addressing now?

④ What is your **Next Step**? (Next experiment) What do you expect?

⑤ How quickly can we go and see what we **Have Learned** from taking that step?

*You'll often work on the same obstac...

Steve

So, that is the real problem! I'm glad we decided to go and observe the process to better understand the problem. We would have wasted time if we had acted on our assumptions.

Example 2: Steve Notices That Robert Needs Cross-Interface Help

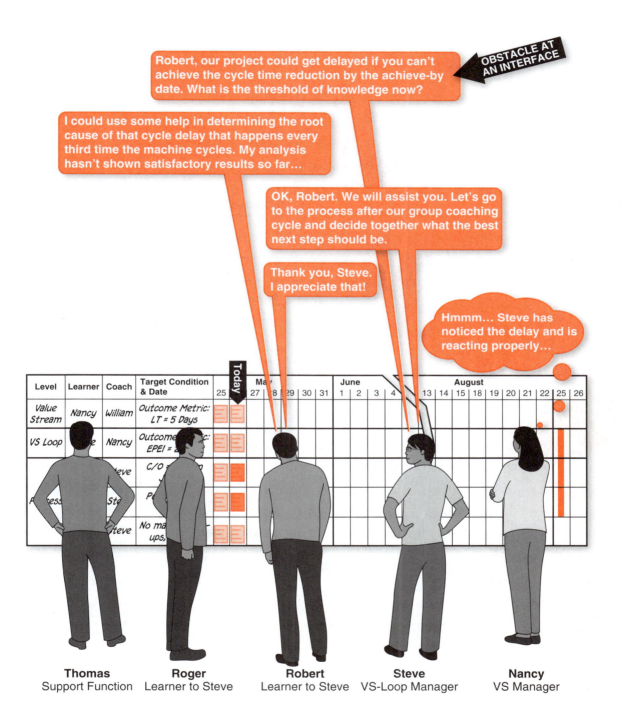

Notice:
Acme Gearbox is Leading and
Managing in the Toyota Way!

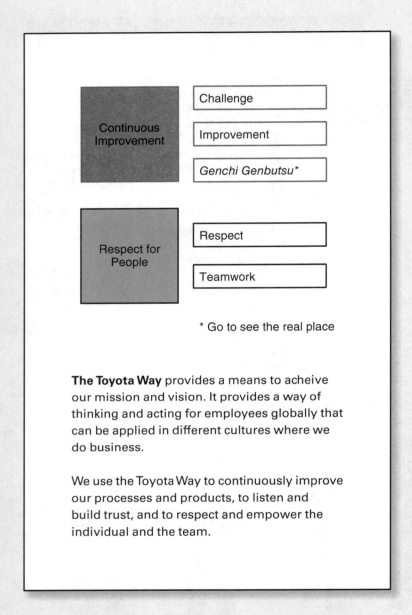

Continuous Improvement

Challenge

Improvement

*Genchi Genbutsu**

Respect for People

Respect

Teamwork

* Go to see the real place

The Toyota Way provides a means to acheive our mission and vision. It provides a way of thinking and acting for employees globally that can be applied in different cultures where we do business.

We use the Toyota Way to continuously improve our processes and products, to listen and build trust, and to respect and empower the individual and the team.

Image adapted from Toyota Motor Corporation, Environmental & Social Report 2003, page 80.
Text adapted from Toyota Motor Corporation, 2007 North American Environmental Report, page 5.

Steve's Coach, Nancy, Participates in the Group Coaching Cycle and Gives Feedback

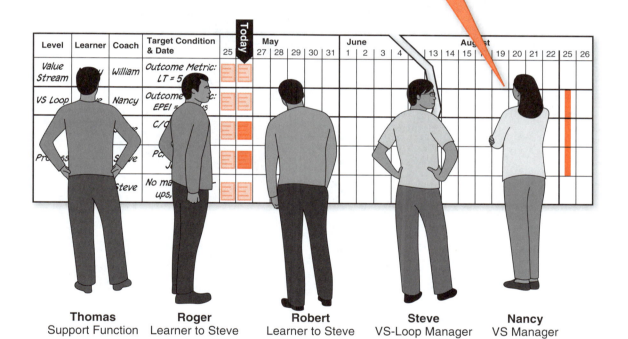

Summary So Far—Expanding Sideways

Now you have seen how the same patterns of the Improvement Kata and Coaching Kata are used to help coordinate and support improvers *horizontally* in an organization.

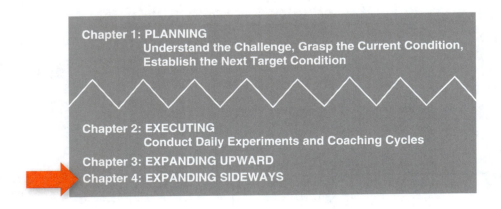

GETTING STARTED AND DEVELOPING YOUR OWN WAY

The Pattern and Practice Routines of the Improvement Kata and Coaching Kata Help You Create a Deliberate Culture

In complex and dynamic markets it often no longer works to have a few individuals making decisions and trying to command and control an organization. In such market conditions, the advantage is often with organizations that adapt, innovate, and continuously improve, at all levels, by mobilizing and coordinating the brainpower of everyone in the organization.

As this book illustrates, the Improvement Kata and Coaching Kata are about teaching a systematic and scientific way of working throughout an organization, to get better at reaching difficult goals. It's a culture-modification process that involves developing new skills and a new mindset through deliberate, coached practice.

By practicing the Improvement Kata and Coaching Kata in chains, as depicted in this book, you are:

- Aligning the organization by creating shared purpose and connection.

- Making the creation of a scientific thinking culture part of normal daily work.

- Creating a shared skillset. Developing capability and power that your organization can utilize to pursue challenging strategic goals.

- Developing a common working language.

- Making innovation happen at every level.

For you—the individual—playing in an orchestra is different than just playing alone. You learn more, achieve more, and you see how you are connected, supported, and empowered by being part of an organization. Probably no human organization will ever be able to function like clockwork, but we humans have the capability to do better than just command and control. In fact, the future may demand it of us.

By building chains of daily coached Kata practice as depicted in this book, you develop capability and power that your organization can utilize to define and pursue its strategic concepts. Ideally, all leaders and managers would apply scientific thinking in their respective roles. **Leaders** work to understand the customer and markets and define the strategic direction of the organization, striving to differentiate the organization from its competitors. **Managers** teach their teams how to navigate effectively (scientifically) in the strategic direction of the organization, by coaching daily practice of the Improvement Kata pattern.

Practicing the Improvement Kata and Coaching Kata throughout an organization helps create situations where great things occur, where brilliant results (large or small) are achieved with positive creative energy. Teams share a way of thinking and working (a "meta skill") that helps them successfully navigate unpredictable paths. They don't propose random solutions and argue about who has the best idea, they argue about the best next experiment. Through practicing the IK and CK, a team is not only proud of its achievements, it is no longer the same. Its way of thinking and doing things, its culture, has shifted.

That is the goal of practicing the Improvement Kata and Coaching Kata.

Begin with the Starter Kata and Progressively Build Your Own System

This workbook gives you a practical, connected picture of what an established Improvement Kata coaching system looks like and how it functions in an organization. At the start of the book we encouraged you to think of the picture this book paints as a challenge to iteratively work toward. The picture helps give some direction to your own deployment/ development process.

Make no mistake, intentionally shifting an organization's culture is a significant undertaking. For instance:

- This is not just about adding techniques on top of the way you currently lead and manage, but rather changing how you lead and manage.

- Leaders and managers will have to be among the first to practice and learn the new skills themselves, before they can coach others.

- To make the pattern of the Improvement Kata a habit, it should be practiced and coached as part of every day's normal work.

- Ultimately, you have to evolve into your own system, based on your practice and experience.

No one can tell you in advance how your deployment will unfold. However, there are fundamental starter routines—the Starter Kata—which are a good place to begin. For more detailed information on how to use and practice the Starter Kata, for both the learner and the coach, please refer to the *The Toyota Kata Practice Guide* (2017, McGraw-Hill).

Just like in sports, music, and other complex skillsets, you begin by practicing some fundamentals. As the patterns of the Starter Kata become somewhat routine you'll begin to understand their elements and how they are related. Then you can move beyond rigidly practicing Kata and build on them, to develop your own style that suits your organization—as long as the basic principles and patterns of the Kata remain.

What characterizes proficient practitioners is the fact that they have learned basic routines to the point that these routines are second nature, and they can focus on interpretation and new combinations that fit the unique characteristics of particular situations—i.e., meta skills.

As it spreads, the effort gets more complex, yet, fortunately, it is always based on the same underlying patterns and structure at all levels of the organization. The fact that the Improvement Kata and Coaching Kata patterns are fractal helps greatly in their deployment.

An Example—Developing Your Own Clarifying Coaching Kata Questions

Let's look at one example of how your practice can evolve beyond a Starter Kata, while maintaining the basic pattern and principles of the Starter Kata: adding your own Coaching Kata questions and guidelines.

As your coaching abilities grow, it's natural to evolve your own coaching style, which includes building on the fundamental five Starter Kata Coaching Kata questions. Of course, any additional questions you come up with should be consistent with the pattern and intention of the Starter Kata (which should remain at the core of your routines).

Begin with the starter five question card shown on page 11. These are the main headings for a coaching cycle. After you do several coaching cycles and get used to what's on that card, you should start adding your own notes and additional clarifying questions, to ask in between the questions on the card. Here's one technique for doing that—make yourself a *folding* question card as shown below. The folded card still fits in your pocket but has space on the unfolded right-hand side to jot down notes and test your own clarifying questions.

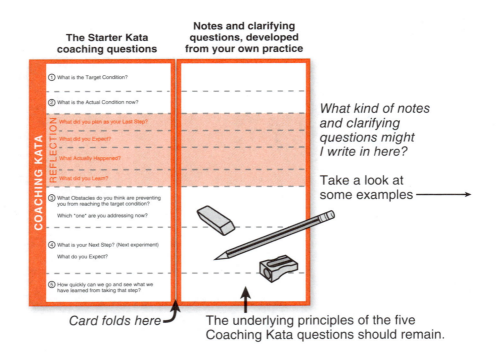

Coaching Kata—Some Example Clarifying Questions

Here are some example notes and clarifying questions to consider and try, simply as thought starters.

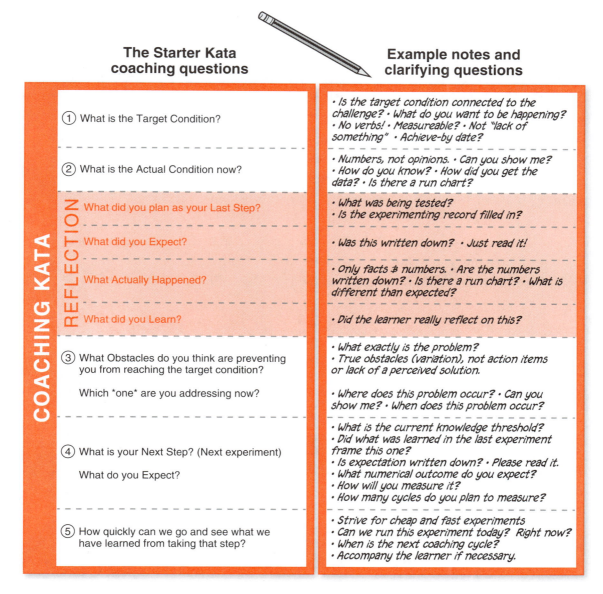

The Starter Kata coaching questions | **Example notes and clarifying questions**

COACHING KATA

① What is the Target Condition?
- Is the target condition connected to the challenge? • What do you want to be happening? • No verbs! • Measureable? • Not "lack of something" • Achieve-by date?

② What is the Actual Condition now?
- Numbers, not opinions. • Can you show me? • How do you know? • How did you get the data? • Is there a run chart?

REFLECTION

What did you plan as your Last Step?
- What was being tested?
- Is the experimenting record filled in?

What did you Expect?
- Was this written down? • Just read it!

What Actually Happened?
- Only facts & numbers. • Are the numbers written down? • Is there a run chart? • What is different than expected?

What did you Learn?
- Did the learner really reflect on this?

③ What Obstacles do you think are preventing you from reaching the target condition?

Which *one* are you addressing now?
- What exactly is the problem?
- True obstacles (variation), not action items or lack of a perceived solution.
- Where does this problem occur? • Can you show me? • When does this problem occur?

④ What is your Next Step? (Next experiment)

What do you Expect?
- What is the current knowledge threshold?
- Did what was learned in the last experiment frame this one?
- Is expectation written down? • Please read it.
- What numerical outcome do you expect?
- How will you measure it?
- How many cycles do you plan to measure?

⑤ How quickly can we go and see what we have learned from taking that step?
- Strive for cheap and fast experiments
- Can we run this experiment today? Right now?
- When is the next coaching cycle?
- Accompany the learner if necessary.

Apply the Improvement Kata to Your Deployment

This is the best deployment advice we can give you—be sure to apply the Improvement Kata pattern to your Improvement Kata deployment. Since no two deployments of the Improvement Kata and Coaching Kata are alike, there is a need to go beyond just planning, to continually experimenting, observing, and adjusting *at the organizational (deployment) level*.

Planning a perfect deployment of new skills is impossible, so it will be important to sense obstacles, problems, and weaknesses as they arise, learn from them, and adapt your deployment accordingly. This is normal and you should determine early on what team of people has the responsibility of overseeing the deployment—conducting regular reflections (you can ask the five Coaching Kata questions here, too)—and introducing deployment course corrections as required. Hopefully you are already thinking, *"Yes, we need to apply scientific thinking to our deployment too!"*

We can also tell you that the gating factor for the speed and range of a deployment is the amount of coaching capability you are able to develop in your organization. You can't really expand further and faster than your managers' coaching ability.

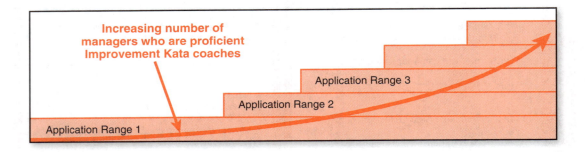

Keep in mind that to be able to coach the Improvement Kata, a manager should first have personal experience with applying the Improvement Kata. Some demonstrated proficiency with the Improvement Kata is ideally required before starting to coach. The skills progression looks like this:

> 3–Able to TEACH scientific improvement thinking as a *coach*
>
> 2–Able to APPLY scientific improvement thinking as a *learner*
>
> 1–AWARE of the pattern of scientific improvement thinking

Practicing IK/CK Saves Managers' Time

The picture we paint of coaching many people in an organization might seem like an overwhelming, time-consuming add-on at first, but you should expect the opposite to soon be the case. That's because, when done right, the Improvement Kata and Coaching Kata unburden managers by replacing some of the reactive, ad hoc activities they normally do.

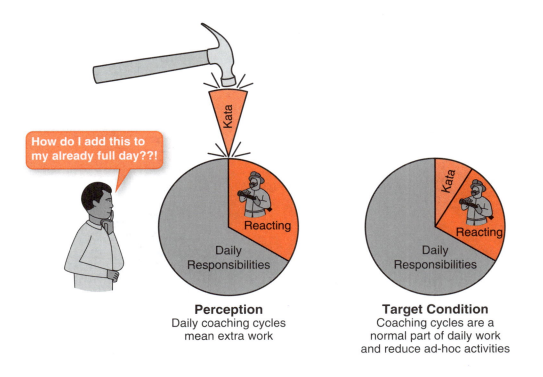

Perception
Daily coaching cycles
mean extra work

Target Condition
Coaching cycles are a
normal part of daily work
and reduce ad-hoc activities

Specifically, practicing a scientific way of working and managing should reduce the amount of time spent in firefighting, unstructured meetings, additional clarifying dialogues due to miscommunication, and unnecessary problem solving. As managers acquire Improvement Kata coaching skill they should expect to free up at least as much time as their coaching cycles take. By better using the capabilities and motivation of their people, a manager should start to experience better results with less energy and time.

The more capability you develop in your teams, the more you can empower and count on them. Instead of pushing your teams, you will feel the *pull* as they strive to achieve target conditions—scientifically—and even meet challenges that may have been considered impossible.

It Helps to Experience the Chain Early On

We have been painting a picture of chains of Kata Coaching in an organization, but there is no substitute for actually experiencing it. The purpose of this book is to set you up to experience the chain of coaching.

Once you have some IK/CK practice underway we suggest that you simulate a chain of Kata coaching as described in this book. Don't wait. You might get some flipchart paper and sketch out a simplified coaching summary board. Gather your practicing colleagues and together go through a chain of coaching cycles as described in Chapter 2, with all practitioners present.

It will not work perfectly and you will find lots of obstacles. However, you will now be far ahead because you'll have learned with the body.

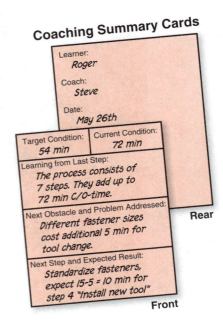

Coaching Summary Cards

Learner:
Roger

Coach:
Steve

Date:
May 26th

Target Condition: *54 min* Current Condition: *72 min*

Learning from Last Step:
The process consists of 7 steps. They add up to 72 min C/o-time.

Next Obstacle and Problem Addressed:
Different fastener sizes cost additional 5 min for tool change.

Next Step and Expected Result:
Standardize fasteners, expect 15-5 = 10 min for step 4 "Install new tool"

Rear

Front

Courage for Your Practice

There is more that we could present here, and we imagine you might like to see more information, examples, and answers from our experience. That might be interesting to read, but it will probably not be of much actual use to you. Engagement in practice that *you* find meaningful and purposeful is the key to skill development, not reading about it. With the picture that this book has now given you in mind, we simply want to say . . .

Why practice the Improvement Kata and Coaching Kata?

→ Because they will simultaneously develop and mobilize your teams!

Best wishes for your practice and for creating effective chains of coaching in your organization. We will be practicing too.

Mike and Gerd

APPENDIX

KEY FORMS

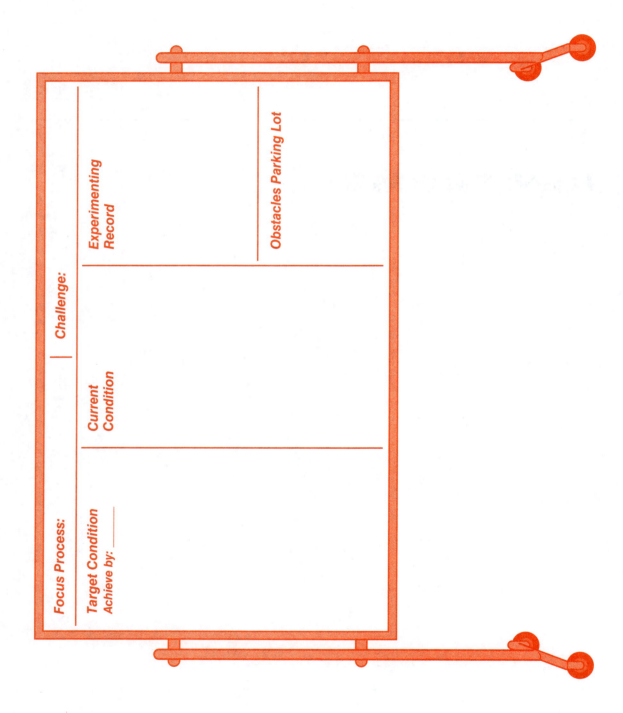

The Improvement Kata Coaching Cycle form, shown rotated, contains the following fields: Focus Process, Challenge, Target Condition (Achieve by:), Current Condition, Experimenting Record, and Obstacles Parking Lot.

COACHING KATA

The Five Questions

(1) What is the **Target Condition**?

(2) What is the **Actual Condition** now?

--------(*Turn Card Over*)--------------▸

(3) What **Obstacles** do you think are preventing you from reaching the target condition?

Which *one* are you addressing now?

(4) What is your **Next Step**? (Next experiment) What do you expect?

(5) How quickly can we go and see what we **Have Learned** from taking that step?

*You'll often work on the same obstacle with several experiments

COACHING KATA

The Five Questions

(1) What is the **Target Condition**?

(2) What is the **Actual Condition** now?

--------(*Turn Card Over*)--------------▸

(3) What **Obstacles** do you think are preventing you from reaching the target condition?

Which *one* are you addressing now?

(4) What is your **Next Step**? (Next experiment) What do you expect?

(5) How quickly can we go and see what we **Have Learned** from taking that step?

*You'll often work on the same obstacle with several experiments

Reflect on the Last Step Taken

Because you don't actually know
what the result of a step will be!

1. What did you plan as your **Last Step?**
2. What did you **Expect?**
3. What **Actually Happened?**
4. What did you **Learn?**

------------------------------>
Return to question 3

Reflect on the Last Step Taken

Because you don't actually know
what the result of a step will be!

1. What did you plan as your **Last Step?**
2. What did you **Expect?**
3. What **Actually Happened?**
4. What did you **Learn?**

------------------------------>
Return to question 3

CC / TC Form	Process:	Coach:	Learner:
Category	**Current Condition**	**Target Condition**	

EXPERIMENTING RECORD (Each row = one experiment)

Obstacle:

Process:

Learner:

Coach:

Date & step	What do you expect + metric		Conduct the Experiment / Do a Coaching Cycle	What happened	What we learned

INDEX

ABOUT THE AUTHORS

Mike Rother

Mike is an engineer, researcher, teacher, and author of the bestselling books *Learning to See* and *Toyota Kata*. He works to develop scientific thinking in individuals, teams, and organizations, shares his findings widely, and has been inducted into the Association for Manufacturing Excellence Hall of Fame.

Gerd Aulinger

Gerd is a researcher, speaker, and management coach who helps leaders develop their people's improvement skills as they simultaneously improve the flow of value to their customers. He views the Improvement Kata and Coaching Kata as part of a holistic management system and is motivated by the way it generates collective experimentation toward challenging strategic goals.

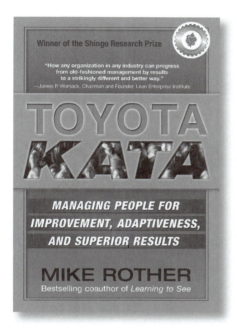
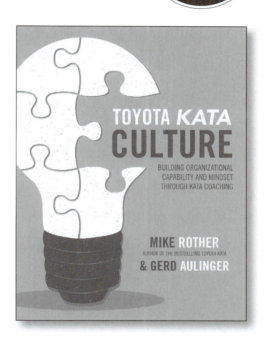